The Successful Lodge:

Best Practices in Freemasonry, by 70 Well Traveled Brethren

Lessons in Nonprofit Leadership

from
Past Grand Master James F. Easterling, Jr.
with David Ferris and Brethren from
Ohio's 21st Masonic District

6623 Press Motivational

Akron

Proceeds from this book go to the Easterling Scholarship.

Founded in 2013, the annual scholarship awards $1,000 to graduating high school seniors who are active in Ohio's 21st Masonic District, who demonstrate a strong will to pursue higher education and have the greatest need.

Visit www.MasonicOH21.net for more details, or see the back of this book for an application.

For bulk copies and fundraising opportunities for your Lodge, please contact the publisher or authors: jimjr1137@neo.rr.com or 6623Press@gmail.com.

The Successful Lodge is a unique manual for Masonic leaders, who operate in a nonprofit environment like no other. From two Past Grand Masters to recently raised Brethren, 70 experienced Freemasons share their advice on making a positive difference in your Lodge.

For the first time, these proven methods of leadership are compiled into a handy book that a motivated Mason might read in one afternoon — then revisit during the rest of his life in Lodge. Experienced line officers discuss communication, planning, management, harmony, ritual, goals, programming, diversity, education programs, member needs, building management, customer expectations, and dozens of other subjects that effective officers and active Brethren need to contemplate.

This diverse anthology of hard-won, battle-tested knowledge can improve your organization this week, next year, and for decades to come.

Methodology/Premise

Thank you for picking up *The Successful Lodge*.

Perhaps you can read it in a single sitting. But — like the valuable lessons inculcated in the several Masonic lectures and charges — you can revisit this expert advice over a lifetime and always take away some fresh wisdom, whether you are an officer working your way toward the East, or you are a rank-and-file member who wants to offer a key idea as your Lodge plans its year.

To produce this book, we asked dozens of accomplished Freemason leaders three deliberately vague, open-ended questions:

What makes a Lodge successful?

What is necessary to have a successful Lodge?

How do you make a Lodge successful?

...and we asked them to answer in any manner they saw fit. 70 of them did.

In this day and age — as it ever was — there is no single magical answer that can make each and every Lodge operate smoothly. And no single course of action can guide a Lodge through each dilemma of leadership, finance, and membership.

With that in mind, we are not offering a single answer. Or a single point of view. Or a uniform set of answers.

Some Brethren answered our questions as we presented them. Some answered the questions with additional, thought-provoking questions. Some offered advice. Some drafted lists. Some told stories. Some delivered anecdotes. Some gave answers you can implement today. Some drew long-term strategies that can guide your Lodge before and after your time in the East.

Every Lodge exists in a unique environment. Each Lodge faces distinct challenges. A financially sound suburban Lodge with an average age of 50 has different needs than a borderline-bankrupt Lodge with a decrepit building and an average age of 65. Some of these answers might not be applicable to your group. Some are.

And, as many Brethren note, not all Masons agree as to what constitutes a successful Lodge. As leaders, that is an issue we need to ask ourselves and our Brethren.

In essence, this book is a guide and a resource. But most of all, it is a survey. So if you see the same point over and over, please consider it important, not redundant.

And if you see an answer only once, please give it serious consideration, as well. Success is uncommon, and often, a minority opinion is marginal, and it seems outlandish — until it suddenly becomes a widely adopted best practice.

Good luck to you, your Lodge, and your Brethren in your Masonic year. We are confident these answers to those questions will help.

Fraternally,

PGM James F. Easterling, Jr., WM David Ferris, and the Brethren of Ohio's 21st Masonic District

Version 1.0. Originally published April 2015.

www.MasonicOH21.net

6623 Press

www.6623Press.com
6623 Press, 6623 Press Motivational, and logos
are trademarks of 6623 Press LLC

Cover design by Christy Carmody, www.christycarmody.com

Graphics by Gerard Dominick
for www.gdesigns-marketing.com

Library of Congress Cataloging-in-Publication Data
Easterling, James F., Jr. and Ferris, David
The Successful Lodge: Best Practices in Freemasonry /
edited by James F. Easterling, Jr. and David Ferris
Pages CM
Includes index

ISBN-13: 978-0692403747 (pbk..: alk. Paper)
ISBN-10: 0692403744
1. Freemasonry. 2. Freemasons—Lodge management
3. Freemasonry—Lodges 4. Leadership
5. Nonprofit organizations
I. Easterling Jr., James F. II. Ferris, David

TABLE OF CONTENTS

Questions for *you*:

What makes a Lodge successful?

What is necessary to have a successful Lodge?

How do you make a Lodge successful?

Ohio's 21ˢᵗ Masonic District

Ohio's 21ˢᵗ Masonic District is home to 28 Lodges. As of July 31, 2014, its population was 6,680 Brethren.

Its oldest active Lodges are Tuscarawas Lodge #59 and Canton Lodge #60, both chartered December 11, 1821.

21ˢᵗ District officers and Worshipful Masters, 2015.

Introduction

By James F. Easterling, Jr.
Past Grand Master of Masons in Ohio (2012-2013)

My father made a statement that changed my life forever, in 1989. He said, "I have joined something very special, that I know would interest you very much." He was very correct.

Never in my life did I think I would find a group of like-minded men, with the same beliefs as myself, who wanted to get to know me and my family, that I could join in helping my community.

After traveling for many years through the State of Ohio and to many different lodges, I have found that the 21st Masonic District (Summit, Stark and Tuscarawas Counties) is unique and diverse. From the rolling hills of rural Tuscarawas County, to the more populated cities of Akron and Canton, and in many small communities alike, Masons from all over these three counties have diverse thoughts about our great fraternity.

Honorable men based this great country on the principles of God, country, patriotism and service to our fellow man. Freemasonry has had a very important part in making America strong and a leader in the world.

To grow as a man and Mason has helped me tenfold, and I thank my father for directing me down this wonderful path.

Fraternally,

James F. Easterling, Jr.
The Grand Lodge of Ohio,
Free and Accepted Masons

Introduction
By David Ferris, WM, Meridian Sun #69

I want to know.

I want to know how it's done. I want to know how it *can* be done. I want to know how to do it well.

So I ask a lot of questions.

What am I talking about?

Everything.

Parenting. Martial arts. Organizational communication. Writing profiles. And, as a first-time WM, Freemasonry.

We should always be looking for more light, no matter what our vocation. Or avocation. And the right question might save us hours — or years — of research and fumbling in the dark.

As I prepared for my year in the East, I asked questions to every Worshipful Master and Past Master I could: What do you wish you knew before you took the big chair? Now that you're in charge, what do you wish you had done six months ago? And I asked questions like the connected trio that form the basis of this book.

As Lodge leaders, we're busy people. Often, we don't know what questions to ask until it's too late. We don't know what angles to consider until the last minute. We don't know what issues to ponder until they are upon us. And no matter how willing our Brethren, those conversations of good advice can be few and far between.

Even at our most pro-active and inquisitive, most of us might have one really valuable conversation of Masonic advice per month. Maybe two. And only so much information fits in your head. Unless you were taking notes, your mentor Past Master probably gave you a great pointer — or ten — that you forgot while you were memorizing the MM obligation. Light is hard to capture, preserve, and pass along. Unless you write it down.

We wrote it down for you.

This book presents 70 multifaceted servings of expert counsel from experienced Brethren who have run a Lodge — or, in some cases, a Masonic District, a Grand Lodge, an Appendant Body, or a business — or contributed more than their share to help their Lodge continue in these trying, changing times.

As you approach the East — or even if you don't have time to serve as an officer now, but you want to contribute to your Lodge — these are the things you need to know about, that you might not consider until it's too late. Leadership. Management. Planning. Communication. Committees. Families. Newsletters. Psychology. Asset allocation. Property management. Income streams. Start thinking about them now. Take some notes. And your year will be better. And so will the years that follow.

This book is not one trestle board. This is a temple full of trestle boards. May they help you draw your own designs for your Lodge.

— Ferris

Notes on Style

In this book, capitalization is a hybrid method based on house styles of the Grand Lodge of Ohio and the Northern Masonic Jurisdiction: "Masonic," "Mason(s)," and "Freemasonry," "Brother," "Brethren," "Worshipful Master," "Lodge," and "Past Master" are always capitalized.

As is standard for most styles, titles are capitalized when they are part of larger construction that constitutes a proper noun ("Secretary John Smith"), but not when they stand alone ("Smith is a former secretary...").

All references to our Brethren, their achievements, and institutions, are made with all due respect. This style is designed to minimize Overenthusiastic Masonic Capitalization; only *you* can prevent OMC.

Opposite page:

This picture was taken April 10, 2013 at Warpole Lodge #176, in Upper Sandusky. Grand Chaplin RWB Tom White and I traveled through a terrible hail and thunderstorm to get there. When we arrived, there was no electric anywhere. We entered the dark Lodge room, and the only thing we could see was this beautiful altar with the lit candles. What a great evening to do degree work, old-school style. It was a great night in Masonry.

— Easterling

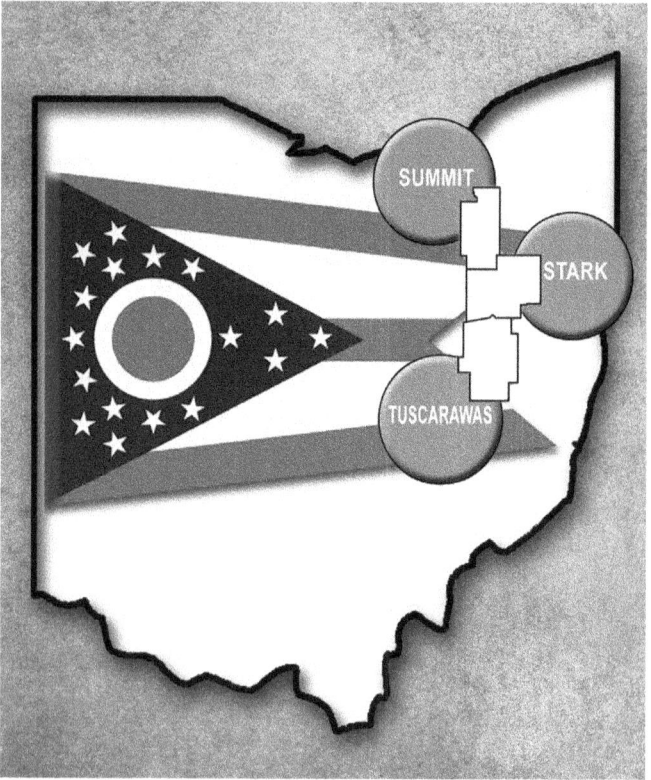

**Ohio's 21st Masonic District:
Summit, Stark, and Tuscarawas Counties.**

Notes on Brethren Titles
Or, "Who Are These Guys?"

Freemasonry is not a contest. All of the Brethren whose opinions are presented here are excellent men with a good head on their shoulders.

Some contributors have served multiple terms as Worshipful Master. Some are not in the progressive officer line, but fill other important roles in their Lodge. Some are first-time WMs. Some are diligently working their way toward the East.

Outside Lodge, some are Marines. We have a retired Federal Marshal. We have CFO's. We have CEO's. Laborers. A painter. Policemen. A carpenter. Teachers. Educators. Authors. Machine operators. Some own a small business. Some own a large business.

In the interest of brevity, we have not included extensive recaps of these Brothers' credentials, titles, careers, and qualifications, in Lodge or out.

Instead, after each Brother's name, no more than two credits follow: his highest title, plus status as a Past/Worshipful Master. Or, if he has not served as WM, his highest place in his Blue Lodge. If we're telling you they have good advice for running your lodge, it's fair to ask whether they have done the job.

The most important title in Masonry is "Brother." And these are the Brethren who find the time to do more than most. We think their words are worth your time; please consider them.

May we always meet on the level.

— Easterling

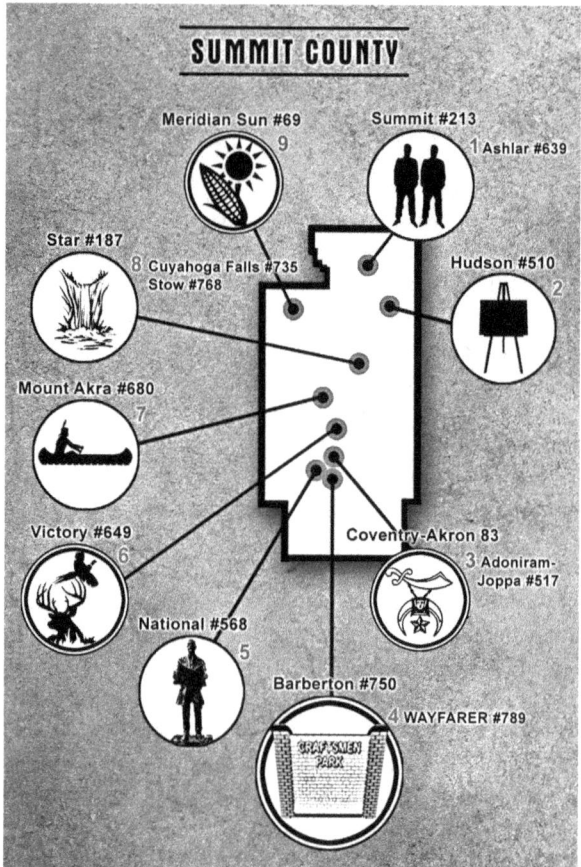

SUMMIT COUNTY

Meridian Sun #69   9   Summit #213

1 Ashlar #639

Star #187

8 Cuyahoga Falls #735
Stow #768

Hudson #510

2

Mount Akra #680

7

Victory #649

6

Coventry-Akron 83

3 Adoniram-
Joppa #517

National #568

5

Barberton #750

4 WAYFARER #789

CRAFTSMEN PARK

1. Twinsburg Temple. 2. Hudson Temple
3. Tadmor Shrine 4. Portage Lakes Temple
5. Barberton Temple 6. Kenmore Temple
7. Old Portage Temple. 8. Cuyahoga Falls Temple
9. Richfield Temple

STARK COUNTY

Conrad #271

William H. Hoover #770

Tubal #551

Clinton #47

Canton #60

Trinity #710
William McKinley #431

1. Alliance Temple 2. Minerva Temple
3. Canton Temple 4. Massillon Temple
5. North Canton Temple

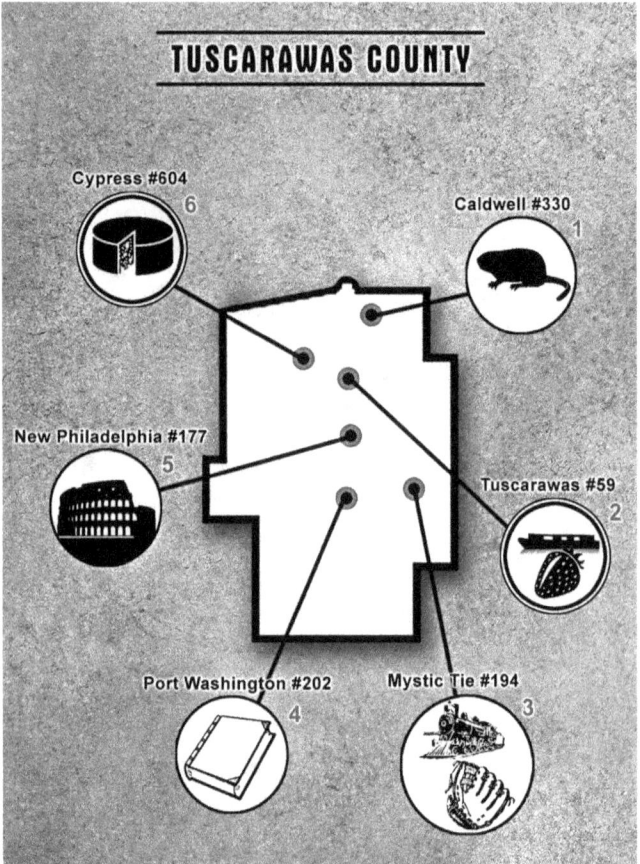

TUSCARAWAS COUNTY

Cypress #604
6

Caldwell #330
1

New Philadelphia #177
5

Tuscarawas #59
2

Port Washington #202
4

Mystic Tie #194
3

1. Bolivar Temple 2. Dover Temple
3. Dennison Temple 4. Gnadenhutten Temple
5. New Philadelphia Temple 6. Strasburg Temple.

YOUR PERSONAL TRESTLE BOARD, PAGE 1:

List some ideas you can mention at your next meeting.

YOUR PERSONAL TRESTLE BOARD, PAGE 2:

List some ideas you think can help your Lodge over the next five years.

Alliance Temple, January 2015. Photo by Easterling.

JIM ADKINS
Brother, National #568

What makes a Lodge successful?

Successful Lodges celebrate the diversity of their membership. Working together, they plan events and activities that bring together men, united under their accepted belief in Brotherhood. These men work together, play together, and believe together that they are making a difference in today's world.

What is necessary to have a successful Lodge?

Growth! When anything stops growing, it dies. Growth sometimes requires change. Today's young men simply have not had the same experience in family life, education, religion, entertainment, and experience as anyone over 30 years old, from past generations.

Contemporary thinking is self-centered and does not emphasize thinking about others first. The human need to belong has depersonalized some of us through the power of technology, allowing anyone to connect without personal contact or commitment.

How do you make a Lodge successful?

Lodges become successful when good leadership involves as many members as possible in an action plan. Leaders must lead by example. The Lodge should make it its business to have more Indians than chiefs. Improving attendance comes from an expectation to understand and live by our obligations (which are binding promises).

MICHAEL J. BAILEY
PDDGM/PM, National #568

I can't think of the true source, but I like to say, "Communication is a wonderful tool — when deployed."

What makes a Lodge successful?

The definition of success is very subjective. To many, success may be just having a place to come for a meeting until they can no longer get around. A successful fraternity enriches their membership with educational programs, a variety of social activities, and opportunities to grow both spiritually and practically. A successful Lodge should be very aware of the makeup of the community in which it exists. A Masonic Lodge has the ability to offer things that other fraternities do not, but often falls short on delivery.

Success starts with the leadership. Do your lodge leaders exhibit successful traits in their personal and professional lives? A great movie quote says, "people follow leaders, not titles" — and that speaks directly to Freemasonry; we have a lot of titles.

A successful Lodge manages it assets prudently and has at least three sources of income. Income streams must be managed and evaluated on a regular basis. The members of the Lodge should feel at ease asking questions about the assets of the Lodge. And they should not made to feel it is none of their business.

A welcoming attitude towards members and guests is also an important component of a Lodge's success. Constant reminders are necessary to make sure that our members are cordial to all whom we have the privilege to encounter at Lodge meetings and functions.

What is necessary to have a successful Lodge?

Communication is the most vital component of any successful organization. There are many ways to communicate with the members, and if we do not do that well, any other efforts will be in vain. If you are a retailer, communicating the value of your product is essential to your store's success.

The most valuable tool Freemasonry has to communicate its message is our members. Unfortunately, often, the members best suited to extol the virtues of our Lodges spend most of their time at Masonic functions, impressing each other. What is necessary for success is to get our truly good leaders to get involved with other civic, charitable, and professional organizations, and to demonstrate their abilities, thereby attracting people to the Lodge.

How do you make a Lodge successful?

You must first become self-aware. You have to be honest in evaluating strengths and weaknesses. If that is what is necessary to become successful, a Lodge must be willing to change.

How do I make my Lodge successful?

I do my best to set an example.

I offer support and assistance to those willing to take advice. My attendance at Lodge functions and meetings demonstrates an interest in my Lodge and its members.

I strive to improve myself, demonstrating that — as in Freemasonry — you must continue in labors, moving steadily toward perfection, knowing all the while I will never attain it.

THE SUCCESSFUL LODGE

CLAUDE BALL
PDDGM/PM, Summit #213

What makes a Lodge successful?

Successful Lodges are careful with those who seek membership, remembering the adage "We make good men better men"; then, through Masonic association, good leaders are developed using Masonic education and experience, with our Masonic lessons.

Finally, those who have promise are encouraged to seek leadership positions in the Lodge. Promising Masons are those who are enthusiastic, have good leadership skills and, most importantly, imagination.

What is necessary to have a successful Lodge?

Imaginative Lodge programs and activities encourage membership participation.

Lodges then endorse the programs set forth by their leaders (officers), encourage them, and offer advice when requested.

Previous leaders (Past Masters) in successful Lodges have an informal organization able to offer encouragement to officers and mentor new members. In successful Lodges, there are no sidelines, because everyone participates!

How do you make a Lodge successful?

As in all successful organizations: Good people achieve great results!

ROBERT J. BECKER, JR.
PM, Meridian Sun #69

For decades, Meridian Sun Lodge paid bills and upkeep on a building it used a handful of days — at most — each month. But it was also home to OES and events from organizations like the Boy Scouts.

Our numbers fell from 400+ to 150, and dues were not enough to cover costs. All funds raised were spent on costs. No fun! Every conversation was about finance and membership. No one wanted to be associated with a failing organization. So we took a hard look at options.

In 2009, Meridian Sun Lodge sold its Temple building to the Village of Richfield. The second floor is home to the Lodge room, and remains exclusively the domain of Meridian Sun. While the downstairs kitchen, facilities are now open to the community, for activities from civic meetings to Kiwanis pancake breakfasts.

In the years prior to selling Meridian Sun's Temple, we had a strategic planning committee, which asked pretty much the same questions.

Over the course of six months or so, we conducted a lot of interviews, brainstorming, and meetings to get answers about how to refine Meridian Sun's formula, to make the Lodge grow and prosper.

What we found for our situation boiled down to a simple Priority List, which created the foundation that must exist for our Lodge to survive and rebuild. This was our five-year strategic plan we set in motion in 2008.

Items 1-4 created the foundation.

Items 5 and 6 are the engine to drive growth.

Item 7 and 8 are the basic fuel for the engine to run, and it gains steam over time.

Once those items were achieved, we were able to add fun stuff other than work. Once we had the membership participation, events like Table Lodges, and Wii nights were held more often, and they were better attended.

The Meridian Sun Priority List:

1. Officer Line: Full, and a vibrant core of officers.

2. Finances: Must be solid. If all we talk about is money, people view the Lodge as a failing organization, and they do not want to become involved.

3. Membership: Obviously, if these numbers dwindle, we would be in trouble. A successful organization attracts more members.

4. Facility: Had to be attractive, well maintained and affordable, in order to be a source of pride; thus, people would want to be associated.

5. Participation of Members: Once items 1-4 were solid, we could focus on having fun. And more members participated in events.

6. Recognized by the Community: Positive word of mouth accumulates due to those who were members, events, and action spread throughout the community, thus attracting more members.

7. Active in the Community: Reinforces #6.

8. Charitable Works: Members and the community rally to support charity, which provides goals for #5 and #6 to achieve.

Best Practices In Freemasonry

J.D. BOOTH
PDDGM/PM, New Philadelphia #177

What makes a Lodge successful?

1. A Lodge in which the officers work together as a team.

2. The officers know what is expected of them, and are aware of what resources are available to them. And they use those resources.

3. The officers work together to accomplish a mutually established, previously established, and well defined goal.

4. The officers are creative, innovative and establish good two-way communications with their members and each other.

5. The Lodge meetings are interesting, enthusiastic. and use the time productively.

What is necessary to have a successful Lodge?

1. An interesting program oriented towards the enjoyment of the members.

2. A program that attracts and encourages members' participation.

3. Membership recognition (personal community accomplishments, service awards, etc.).

4. Programs that encourage attendance and membership.

5. Meetings that make the members view attendance as time well spent.

6. An atmosphere that promotes a warm and welcome feeling for all members.

How do you make a Lodge successful?

1. You put the good of the Lodge ahead of any personal motives.

2. You encourage all the officers to do their best by working to set an example.

3. Help all officers to do their best by showing a personal interest in their accomplishments and offering appropriate assistance if necessary.

4. You should always be aware of ways that might improve the Lodge.

5. Look to the future, not to the past. Do not repeat previous mistakes.

6. Do not be afraid to make changes that will improve the Lodge.

7. Maintain a positive and enthusiastic attitude in all matters.

8. Treat all members with a concerned attitude. Maintain good relationships.

9. When setting goals or planning events, involve all the officers, so they share in the ownership of all success.

GORDON BROOME
PM, William H. Hoover #770

To make a Lodge successful, a Lodge must get members to commit to some activity, whatever that may be.

Only through some commitment on behalf of the individual will he gain camaraderie with other Lodge members. And this, then, will allow him to feel that he is a part of something he values, and feel accepted.

He might, then, explore other activities, even taking an office in the Lodge, or some involvement in other Lodge activities.

It still takes someone in the Lodge who can motivate people to accomplish this.

Activities must be meaningful, enjoyable, exciting, and purposeful. Whatever that activity is, involvement is the key.

It may take a concerted effort by more than one person or more than one time to get that commitment. But any successful Lodge is one that is not only active, but its members are *Brothers* who work together for the betterment of Freemasonry and feel they are part of a proud organization.

THE SUCCESSFUL LODGE

JIM BRUMBAUGH
PM, Mount Akra #680

What makes a Lodge successful?

In my mind, a successful Lodge is one that is active in their community. And the area around the Lodge feels that the members are included with community events. We are a civic and fraternal organization; Freemasons should be seen as leaders in their respective communities.

What is necessary to have a successful Lodge?

To have a successful Lodge, the members must be informed about what is going on. Active communication with their members. The Master and secretary should be known by their members. If a poll of inactive members was taken, they should at least say they are receiving a bulletin or some regular communication to the events.

How do you make a Lodge successful?

Don't assume that the Brother next to you is going to do the job. Introduce yourself. Make the new member feel welcome. Tell the member that has not been in Lodge it is good to see them.

JEFFERY BURTON
PM, Wayfarer #789

What makes a Lodge successful?

A group of dedicated men or Masons that have a common goal and are willing to make sacrifices to achieve that goal. Growth of its members as individuals and as active members in the community. Growth of new members to keep the fraternity strong.

What is necessary to have a successful Lodge?

Dedicated Brethren who are firm in the code, yet fair. Who are open to change that will attract new members, as well as keeping the current ones active.

How do you make a Lodge successful?

As an individual, be true to yourself and all your Brothers.

As a fraternity, let the Lodge be seen as a valuable asset to the community. This will attract new interest in the fraternity and allow for growth.

Listen to your Brothers. And be open to new ideas.

Also, sometimes, by the grace of God, it just happens.

THE SUCCESSFUL LODGE

STEPHEN COLTON
PDDGM/PM, Star #187

What makes a Lodge successful?

What is necessary to have a successful Lodge?

There are a number of factors that have to be in place to have a successful Lodge.

A dedicated and motivated corps of officers is the heart of it all.

The WM should be a good organizer, planner, and delegator. He needs to start developing those skills in his earliest appointment in the line.

The Lodge secretary should also be a strong assistant and supporter for the WM.

For that to happen, there have to be frequent officer meetings, either after a stated meeting or called meetings, at a local coffee house or some site other than the Lodge.

Wives can — and should —be included.

There should be an agenda, and goals should be set. Who is going to give the next lecture or charge? Brainstorm for ideas for special activities. Who will head a committee? Who will perform the various functions? Checklists have to be made — and kept current.

When a Lodge plans an activity it should, if successful, become an annual event and not be a one-shot thing.

A Lodge that only holds stated and special meetings can't survive much longer. Most younger guys have active and busy lives. Sitting in meetings that offer no variety or involvement probably won't hold their interest for long.

Best Practices In Freemasonry

Inter-Lodge activities should be encouraged.

How do you make a Lodge successful?

Our average age is around, I think, 68. At that point, energy and creative juices seem to slow down. Maybe the key is to change how we get new members. We can't advertise for members, but we can be more "aggressive" in informing friends and neighbors about what the fraternity offers.

To do that, we must be sure of what the fraternity does offer, have booklets available to hand out, and invite potential members to Lodge social functions.

We need to use the community newspapers to advertise events.

Most of those activities have to fall to the younger members, because they and their peer groups are our future.

A passing thought:

When I was a young officer, our secretary — WB Cliff Mason, with whoever was sitting in the East — would have short gatherings after Lodge closed, at a local restaurant, for a planning session. I think more was accomplished during those officer group meetings than any sessions at Lodge.

Maybe we got to know each other better and felt we could let our hair down a bit. Whatever it was, it worked. The bonds that formed were obvious to the Brethren who came to Lodge. Attendance was good. Then again, that was a different time.

Barberton Temple, January 2015. By Easterling.

ALLEN CORBETT
WM, New Philadelphia #177

What makes a Lodge successful?

Active membership by old and young members alike. Regular attendance. And willingness to participate in roles, to secure the future of the Lodge.

What is necessary to have a successful Lodge?

Same as above. In addition, these members taking an active role in recruiting without solicitation. Having young members replace the elderly in the Lodge is absolutely vital.

How do you make a Lodge successful?

I volunteer and participate as much I can and assist wherever I can to help the Lodge be successful.

The Successful Lodge

MATTHEW COWGER
PM, Star #187

What makes a Lodge successful?

What is necessary to have a successful Lodge?

Officers that are interested in doing good work. They communicate with each other, show up for meetings, and take an interest in the new members.

Interesting meetings, not just reading of the minutes.

Lodge education is very important.

Sound finances.

And not all Past Masters in line. Let the "new" guys grow and run with the ball.

We need a FC Team Leader that is responsible for lining up workers and getting them to practice with the officers. Or a Traveling Valley FC team with their own uniforms. I think we drop the ball with new members when we don't portray good degrees. We want them to be so impressed with good work that they want to come back and participate. There is so much to learn and apply to our lives.

How do you make a Lodge successful?

I'm guilty of being a PM who stays in line, not because I can't let go, I feel it's more out of necessity. I always attend meetings when I'm in town, I travel 4-6 days a week for work. I'm there for all degree work and help the WM or anyone else who needs it. I love my Brothers and wish I could do more for the fraternity. We need to be good mentors for each other, young or old, in Lodge and in life.

GLENN CUSTER
Brother, Mount Akra #680

What makes a Lodge successful?

What is necessary to have a successful Lodge?

Active participating members.

How do you make a Lodge successful?

More activities for members.

More activities for members and guests.

Making people feel welcome.

A booklet of all Lodge members, with phone and addresses of the members Lodge.

HAL DILL
PDDGM/PM, Clinton #47

What makes a Lodge successful?

The buy-in and participation of the membership in a clear, concise, and well communicated plan that is based on a long-term vision of where the Lodge as a whole wants to be, in say five years.

Then one-year short-term plans, all geared to achieving the longer goal.

A successful Lodge goes beyond stated meetings and ritual work. There exists an enthusiasm and pride among the membership that they were a part of — and contributed to — the success of the Lodge and its programs. The members are engaged.

What is necessary to have a successful Lodge?

Effective leadership, not necessarily from the officers. Not all leaders are ritualists. And not all ritualists are leaders.

There must be a clear, consistent vision that is well communicated.

The best thought-out plans are useless if not acted upon.

We are in the people business, and people support what they help to create. There must be a culture of inclusion, where every Brother has a place and a purpose, and every idea and opinion is valued.

How do you make a Lodge successful?

By participating and supporting the Lodge and its members in a positive manner.

To be a resource for the members without pushing my ideas as the only option. Recognizing that everyone has ideas.

When a Lodge wishes to move from point A to point B, there are many paths that will get to point B. It is not of utmost important that my way is the right way, but which path makes the Lodge most successful *while involving the most members.*

I can also act as a mediator to help resolve differences and gain support for new ideas and endeavors.

THE SUCCESSFUL LODGE

STEVE DILLEY
WM, William McKinley #431

I believe that depends on your definition of success for a Lodge. I believe success comes from maintaining and retaining members. Also having good and interesting stated meeting programs.

Necessary components would be as follows:

1. A strong LEO who reaches out to new members.

2. A strong philosophy for the officers, which includes personal conduct guidelines, as well as rules for personal conduct outside of the Lodge.

3. A good secretary who understands that the communications are the lifeblood of the Lodge, and who encourages the Brethren to travel and see that our fraternity is much larger than just their own Blue Lodge room.

Making a Lodge successful is the responsibility of each Brother, but largely lies with the master. You can gauge the pulse of a Lodge by who is governing that Masonic year.

If the master is forthright and earnest in his dealings with each officer, and he makes sure to have them aware of requirements as well as expectations of each station, he can expect to have a successful Lodge — as well as a great year.

Before my year in the East, I asked many Past Masters about their year and how successful and or unsuccessful they were. They all replied the same way: "Plan, plan, plan — and when you think you have it all worked out, plan some more!"

I'm not much of a writer, but I hope it helps. See you in the Lodge room.

THE SUCCESSFUL LODGE

BILL DIXON
Past Potentate, Tadmor Shrine

I don't know that I am the best Brother to answer any of your questions at this point, but I'll give it a shot based on some things I've learned.

In my experience what makes a Lodge — or any group — successful is a sense of common purpose among a group of like-minded individuals. Individuals will have differing ways of accomplishing things, but they must all have a common purpose to pursue. It is up to leadership to divine what that purpose is.

What is most necessary is for all of the individuals to have a spirit of forgiveness for each other. With the many differing opinions, individuals must forgive each other for the times they may not have governed their passions while working toward the common purpose.

How I make my Lodge successful is by maintaining my membership and doing what I can when I can. Whatever it is, it should not be ridiculed by a Brother. More Brothers ridicule and complain than actively participate in all of the Lodge activities.

With all of the opportunities Freemasonry offers, one has to chose the direction he may wish to go in a Masonic career. We should encourage Brothers that have made a choice, and we should celebrate their choice.

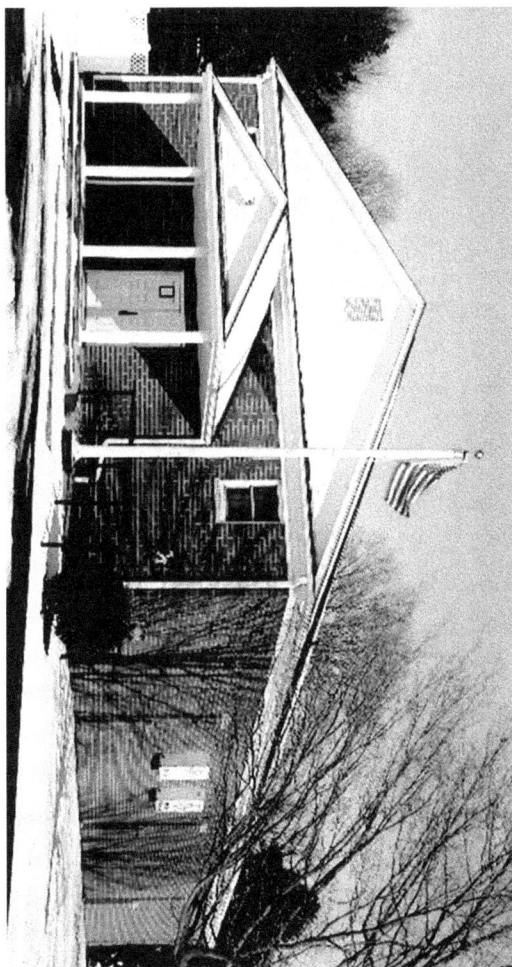

Bolivar Temple, February 2015. Photo by Easterling.

GARY DRESSLER
Secretary, Canton #60

Programs!

A few years ago, we had a WM who worked hard to get interesting programs for our stated meetings. Attendance increased during that year. And then the attendance started dropping off when the following WMs were not as interested in presenting quality programs.

BEST PRACTICES IN FREEMASONRY

JAMES F. EASTERLING, JR.
PM, National #568
Past Grand Master, Grand Lodge of Ohio, F. & A.M.

What makes a Lodge successful?

• Having men who have the same beliefs, and the same interest in our communities, who are committed to banding together as a great influence for the positive.

• To not just sit on your hands at any function; rather, to participate in all activities.

• To help those less fortunate, and always be ready to help in times of need.

What is necessary to have a successful Lodge?

• Members with no agenda.

• Programs of interest to its members and their families.

• Communication.

• Ability to look forward, for long-range planning.

How do you make a Lodge successful?

• Do what needs to be done.

• Promote within the Lodge and in my community.

• Show people that Freemasonry does make a difference.

• **"Together we can..."**

JOHN EVANS, JR.
PM, Meridian Sun #69

Here is how the Great Architect used my year as WM to turn Meridian Sun around.

Short version:

It's all in the degrees.

Long version:

1. Pray

Implore non-attending members to pray as well

2. Peace and Harmony

Determine what is causing dissension.

In 2006, we had a membership crisis and a financial crisis. A large enough crisis that we were supposed to be item #2 on the meeting to rescue the Summit Masonic complex, but that meeting's discussion never made it to us.

So, in my Past Masters' planning meeting, I promised to merge with another Lodge if the line was not filled, or sell the temple if it was.

The members stepped up to fill the line, so I worked on selling the temple, to solve the financial issue.

Don't be afraid to use the gavel to rap down long-winded members during meetings, and to keep it flowing.

3. "Best to work and best agree"

Set others up for success.

Choose committee members carefully. I knew the temple sale would take longer than my term, so committee members were chosen carefully. I also worked with the upcoming masters to make sure that this committee would not change in their years.

Not only did we come up with a fair deal in selling the temple, but we ended up with a new member. He was a member of the local council during the sale, and he became a Brother after the sale. Brother Wheeler is now our current SW, but is personally responsible for at least three other new members over the subsequent years.

4. Communicate

Wise council to junior officers.

Trestle board where the workman can see: newsletter, emails, phone tree, etc.

5. Focus on the tenets.

With financial issues no longer consuming meetings, we were able to focus on Brotherly Love, Relief and Truth.

Social events are key. Even failures. I attempted to stage a Masonic themed trip to Washington, D.C., but did not get enough to sign up. However, just talking about it in the newsletter created interest in the Lodge from non-attending members. Some of the non-attending members became attending members and brought new candidates with them. Unfortunately for other Lodges, we gained members by demit as well.

This was my main focus. Everything else was focused on how to obtain it and keep it.

STEVEN FANNIN
WM, Coventry-Akron #83

I hope my responses can be of genuine help to Freemasonry. This is a genuinely meaningful effort and one that is overdue, in my opinion.

What makes a Lodge successful?

Masonry is, at its heart, a brotherhood.

Adherence to the core values of Brotherhood and fellowship makes for a successful Lodge. Especially in an age of declining membership and waning levels of activity, even a small-but-dedicated group of close-knit Brothers can change the entire picture and outlook of a Lodge.

What is necessary to have a successful Lodge?

A dedicated core of officers who work well together, communicate openly, and work with a sense of mutual respect and appreciation goes a long way toward achieving a strong sense of unity and Brotherhood.

This cooperation can be further highlighted by other, dependable groups. Whether it is a dedicated social group, a well-rehearsed Fellowcraft team, or a group of Brothers who are ready to attend funeral services, a sense of community and dependability is critical for each and every Lodge.

How do you make a Lodge successful?

I think it is important to establish and foster a sense of community and interdependency in Lodge. Mass emails, regular phone calls from the master, telephone chains, and regular social events that involve family and friends help develop Masonry into a community rather than a chore.

Masonry needs to be an extension of our lives and ourselves, and it will be a place Brothers *want* to go, rather than a place they feel they *should* go.

As master of a Lodge, you should schedule a broad-ranging — but not overly ambitious — social calendar. And you should do that while also communicating regularly and openly with the Brethren. It fosters a sense of involvement and unity. Above all, it is important to stay engaged and not get discouraged by minor setbacks or challenges.

THE SUCCESSFUL LODGE

RAZA FAYYAZ
SW, William McKinley #431

What makes a Lodge successful?

Let's face it: The majority of the candidates become interested in Masonry due to its aura of mystery, secrecy and tradition. They are anxious to learn something profound and something new and be better and successful.

So whenever a Lodge gets into the habit of fulfilling these cravings — either through an educational program, a meeting, or through some other event — that Lodge becomes a successful Lodge.

What is necessary to have a successful Lodge?

Some of the ingredients to have a successful Lodge are:

• To do something fun rather than just hearing the minutes, paying the bills, and eating the refreshments.

• To have educational programs because they teach something awesome, and not because we have to fulfill the Grand Lodge's requirements.

• To give members the feeling of progress and advancement by holding candid discussions about Freemasonry.

How do you make a Lodge successful?

I continuously engage in discussions with my Brothers about Esoteric Freemasonry, which can be very addictive.

Since we cannot have these kind of discussions with anyone outside the Lodge, we keep wanting to come back to the Lodge to talk more. These discussions makes us feel as if we belong to a very special Brotherhood and help the Lodge to be successful at the same time.

THE SUCCESSFUL LODGE

DAVID FERRIS
WM, Meridian Sun #69

What makes a Lodge successful?

How do you make a Lodge successful?

So much of Freemasonry involves our mysterious oral tradition that we fall into the habit of never writing down *anything*.

Masonic tradition informs us: Nothing causes a greater stir in a Lodge than a trestle board with no designs.

I carry a pocket-sized notebook with me at all times, so I can write down reminders and update my many to-do lists.

Communicate. Plan. Write it down.

Have an agenda. Write down your schedule. Stick to it.

Let people know in advance. Remind them.

For my year in the East, I adopted the slogan, "Freemasonry doesn't grow on trees."

The phrase began as a joke. But over time, I realized it was a truth that is worth repeating: If you have a Master Mason Degree planned for Wednesday the 14th, you can't just announce it on the 7th, then show up at the Lodge a week later, go out back, and pluck some Masonry off a tree behind the temple. There is no Freemasonry tree.

As you know, mounting a Master Mason Degree requires two dozen Brothers, two hours, and plenty of practice and coordination. And if you don't set it up weeks in advance — and produce & circulate some written notes in the process — the ceremony probably won't be impressive.

That said, correct Freemasonry *is* the result of process that is much like growing a crop. Plan in advance, with an eye on future weeks and seasons. If you need bushels of corn in the Fall, you don't start planting in the late summer. Similarly, if you have a newly obligated EA, and you know you'll need to hold a Master Mason degree in two months, start drafting your Fellowcraft team now.

What is necessary to have a successful Lodge?

If you want a Lodge to run smoothly, the officers need to buy in. They have to feel ownership.

Officers need to realize: As they work, they are already filling their own trestle board, not just slaving away on someone else's designs.

Officers should understand: Their time in the line is a seven-year training program, not unlike a college degree.

In the classic motivational handbook *How to Win Friends and Influence People*, Dale Carnegie explains his third principle in his Fundamental Techniques in Handling People: "Arouse in the other person an eager want."

As WM, are you ordering around your officers, or are you helping them identify and achieve their goals? Do your officers know what they need to do, and do they *want* to do it? As leader, are you helping them develop the desire to work and work well?

They might not realize it, but everything your officers do every year will make their year easier.

Every officer should pay due attention to his long-term needs as a future WM. That mindfulness will help him keep his progress on track.

It's easy to put off learning lectures and charges — we're all busy, and none of us has the time to learn a lecture. But, to paraphrase MW Brother Benjamin Franklin, "Never put off to next year what you can memorize today." Your year in the East will be easier and consume less time if you don't have to spend it memorizing new ritual.

As WM, you can put your head down and concentrate on getting through your year. But when you make your year about your entire team, you're setting up your Lodge for success in the next decade — and beyond.

Canton Temple, January 2015.
Photo by Easterling.

JIM FIDLER
PDDGM/PM, William McKinley
#431 and William H. Hoover #770

The best Lodges have three things in common: A good secretary, a good treasurer, and a group of Past Masters who are interested in seeing that the Lodge does the best it can.

The best Lodges are those that concentrate on the ritual work and setting up their financial and administrative structures. I am not saying that the best ritualists or the best financial managers are necessarily the best Masons, but from what I have seen, the most successful Lodges are those where the members care about the way other Masons and members of the public perceive them. If a Lodge cares about the way that others look at it, it will be a Lodge that is active, energized, and significant in the community.

STEVEN R. FLAUGHERS
Brother, Adoniram-Joppa #517

What makes a Lodge successful?

A Lodge is only as successful as what each Mason brings to the Lodge.

The Lodge is comprised of members bringing something unique to the Lodge, whether it be ideals, information, lessons, history, life lessons, education etc. Not only in the craft — which is very important, and I feel being lost as each member of the older generation dies — but also in life. Many of us younger Masons did not have a father figure — or grandfathers — for one reason or another. And it is where young men are going astray in large quantities.

What is necessary to have a successful Lodge?

Instruction and direction, for getting the name out there. There is nothing wrong with good fellowship and eating refreshments, but there needs to be more substance.

What makes men want to come back, what makes it more alluring to the younger generation to want to become a Mason — and most importantly, remain an *active* Mason?

Programming is important, thinking outside of the box — and by that, I mean not just a table Lodge, or wearing a hula shirt. But for example, National Lodge and their fried bologna sandwich stand: We need to be seen more in the community.

So perhaps adopt a highway.

Perhaps partnering with local college fraternities — they need community service hours and are required to get them. We WANT to do them. So why not connect on that level?

How do you make a Lodge successful?

You get out of it what you put into it.

From the time a member comes in and is raised, it seems like we raise them, then advise, "Well... Come back."

It's a crap shoot if they get engaged or disappear and become another résumé builder or ring flasher.

Each Lodge needs to have a comprehensive program to engage each new Master Mason. If they come through and have no *true* friends, then they may not come back. But if they are good friends and Brothers and have shared experiences with them (see the above answers about doing more as Masons), they are likely to come back often.

MARK J. GOLD
WM, William McKinley #431

What makes a Lodge successful?

A successful Lodge, in my opinion, is a Lodge that has 5 to 10% of its membership, on average, at a regular stated meeting.

What is necessary to have a successful Lodge?

1. To have a successful Lodge, you need to have a strong corps of officers willing to do the job that they are assigned, show up regularly, and do their job with enthusiasm. When the officers get along with each other and perform their duties correctly, it demonstrates Brotherhood that all can see. This will promote attendance.

2. The Past Masters need to support the officers, not try and lead them. In our Lodge, we believe that our Masters are trained well enough to lead the Lodge in their own way, not someone else's. The biggest strength in our fraternity is the diversity of our membership, so we need to capitalize on the premise that every member has something to offer that is beneficial to the craft.

3. Respect *all* Masons the same regardless of rank, purple aprons, or anything else.

I have heard in passing outside in the ante room, "So is this section of the page where the royalty signs in."

That is a disturbing thought, that some of the Brethren don't feel as important as the rest.

We are taught that we are all equal as Master Masons, so as we climb the ranks through the fraternity, we should recall what is said to the senior warden when he is installed — and never forget it.

4. Learn from the elders of the Lodge: Ask them questions. Talk to them every chance you get; they enjoy it, and a time will come when you can't. I have learned so much from them, and I treasure the time I spent with the ones that have passed.

I could go on all day, but I believe that these four items are a good start.

How do you make a Lodge successful?

I try and offer my membership a diverse docket of programs outside of what is required.

In other words, I mix it up a little: I'm serious when I need to be. I make them laugh. I make them think. But most of all, I make them speak.

I like interactive programs that involve all of them. It gets real old real fast when Brethren are being lectured to. Sometimes its necessary, but most of the times, its not.

I try and think of programs that will interest all my Brethren. And believe me: that can be difficult, but I have done it on many occasions. I let them know that I care about them and their family, that we are a family, and when one hurts, we all hurt.

I did something this year that, to my knowledge, has never been done in our Lodge: In our stated meetings, I had a guest in the East, sitting to my left for the evening. I chose members that I would call unsung heroes in our Lodge: our tyler, our master of ceremonies, and other Brethren that may never sit in the East as master, but have contributed greatly to our Lodge.

Last, I never allowed peace and harmony to escape our Lodge. If things started to look like they could go wrong, I steered the Lodge away from the rocks.

GUST GOUTRAS
PDDGM/PM, William McKinley #431

What makes a Lodge successful?

A Lodge is successful when *all* the Brothers are involved in the business, work, and social activities of the Lodge, especially the various committees and degree work of the Lodge.

Every Brother should be on at least one active committee, i.e. finance, relief, ritual, visitation, investigation, etc. Three or five active Brothers — or many times, just the Worshipful Master — *should not* be doing everything.

Committees should meet regularly, perhaps quarterly, before a stated Meeting, to encourage attendance and interest. The members should take turns in giving periodic committee reports to the Lodge.

People who have an ownership interest in any organization tend to be most active.

What is necessary to have a successful Lodge?

Everyone must feel that they have a purpose and function when attending Lodge.

If a Brother is just going to sit on the sidelines and listen to the same agenda over and over, he is going to lose interest, and he is going to stop coming. Look around you, many already have.

How do you make a Lodge successful?

I would like to say the officers need to do that, but that is really not true. Officers are being moved through the line too quickly, and are often overwhelmed, even when they are repeats. I think you have to use the Past Masters, but in a more dedicated and focused manner.

You need a Past Master on every committee, and not just on the sidelines kibitzing or criticizing the newer officers. The PM should not to be in charge of the committee; instead, he should be the WM's representative, or a resource to answer questions. Even PMs will not show up unless they have a purpose.

In conclusion: Give every man a job and let him know that his job is important to the Lodge by having him report on it.

Do not make a handful of zealous Brothers do all the work. You will quickly burn them out and lose them.

Cuyahoga Falls Temple, January 2015.
Photo by Easterling.

JOSHUA GROVE
PM, Victory #649

What makes a Lodge successful?

It is absolutely true that you only get out of something what you put into it. That is part of a Lodge's success, finding the right mix of individuals with the right skill set, who are able to put those skills to work for the Lodge.

What is necessary to have a successful Lodge?

A Lodge must communicate well. Without communication, there is no way that members or visitors will attend.

Also, a Lodge must have a niche, a gimmick, that sets it apart from the other Lodges. This can be their degree work, a special fundraiser or a Fellowcraft team that is at the ready to help other Lodges. Whatever it is, when a Lodge finds that niche, they are set.

How do you make a Lodge successful?

As a member, you have to be willing to put effort into a Lodge. You have to see the benefits of your work. There is not always a reward or pat on the back, so we have to look for the reward of a job well done. If I, as a member, cannot help the Lodge in some way, the Lodge is less successful. A chain is only as strong as its weakest link.

THE SUCCESSFUL LODGE

JOHN D. GUSTAFSON
PDDGM/PM, Cuyahoga Falls #735

What makes a Lodge successful?

I believe a Lodge is successful, simply, when members depart Lodge feeling better as a result of having attended.

What is necessary to have a successful Lodge?

Brotherly Love, a passion for Freemasonry, and focused accomplishment.

How do you make a Lodge successful?

A personal commitment, as a member, to being an active member.

It's not about a few members doing a lot; it's about a lot of members doing a bit.

WILLIAM HADDOW
SW, Mount Akra #680

What makes a Lodge successful?

Participation by all members, not just the Past Masters and the progressive line.

What is necessary to have a successful Lodge?

Participation by members in community events, Lodge events, and especially Lodge meetings.

How do you make a Lodge successful?

Get everyone involved and excited.

Ask the questions, "What made you want to be a Mason in the first place?"

Did you become a Mason to just send in your annual dues and not attend a single stated meeting? Did you achieve what you set out to achieve when you became a Mason?

To be successful, I think we need to be more involved in charitable work, and more involved in the communities.

Success isn't just limited to passing the inspection and doing good degree work.

EARL HALL
Brother, Mount Akra #680

What makes a Lodge successful?

Going back to the original Masonic form. We are all Brothers no matter how many awards, certificates and ranks we have, it all goes back to being stewards of mankind. We must help one another and we must show compassion for one another.

What is necessary to have a successful Lodge?

Having the members feel welcome and wanted each and every time they enter any Lodge. When someone misses a couple meetings someone should call them and find out if they need help and they are missed at Lodge. Stop all cliques in the Lodges, and stop all the politicking which makes many feel not wanted. When a Brother does wrong he should be accountable for negligent actions.

How do you make a Lodge successful?

A new Brother should be assigned a mentor which would be an active Mason to be there to answer all questions, discussions and help in learning Masonry. He should never be left alone to fend for himself and should always have a shadow for support.

DAVID HOPKINS
DDGM/PM, William H. Hoover #770

I believe that in order for a Lodge to be successful, you need the three P's:

A Purpose, Plan, and Priorities.

Purpose:

What I mean by a Purpose is a unified reason why you exist. While the Grand Lodge establishes this for the jurisdiction, each Lodge should have a unified purpose locally.

I realize that our Masonic principles lay the foundation for our universal purpose and mission as a fraternity. But the local Lodge should put something in place that defines them in their community. Some businesses write mission statements that encapsulate why they are here.

For an individual, this is like "knowing who you are." Having this established and well understood by the Lodge, while keeping in line with the mission of the Grand Lodge, can go a long way to directing what the Lodge does. So many times, I hear Brother not able to state, in a clear and succinct manner, the reason why their Lodge is here. They don't know their purpose, which makes much of their efforts directionless and ineffective.

THE SUCCESSFUL LODGE

Plan:

A strategic plan, developed by the leadership of the Lodge and concurred by the membership, provides direction for the efforts of the Lodge.

A business without a plan is destined for failure. The plan will define the success strategy for the Lodge.

The plan cannot be just for a Masonic year; rather, it should be for a minimum of five years. (That is a start.)

The plan should support the purpose and mission of the Lodge, and provide specific and measurable goals. These goals do not only have to be organic in nature. They can be external to the Lodge, but can benefit others (e.g. community-focused).

Putting our Lodge membership on point to establish a Masonic success plan, with responsibility for execution on them, gives meaning to membership.

The plan must be aggressive enough to challenge the Lodge to grow (I don't mean just in numbers), but realistic enough to be achievable. The "SMART" principle is a great guide. (The management-development acronym Specific, Measurable, Assignable, Realistic, Time-related.)

Priorities:

This is the tough one. In order for Lodges (and individual Masons, for that matter) to succeed, they must be willing to make success a priority.

Individual Masons must be willing to make Freemasonry — and supporting the Lodge's Purpose and Plan — a priority in their life. It means committing to coming to the Lodge events and participating in the Lodge functions and its success plan should be an integral part of their life. Whether that is four hours per month, or one day per month, or whatever the commitment, it should be a priority. If you want a return on an investment, you must be willing to invest.

Successful Lodges are those that have implemented the above strategy. Some have not written this down, but the leadership has diligently communicated this strategy. However, when the purpose and plan are written and established, and the membership is on board to make success a priority, it always seems to work.

THE SUCCESSFUL LODGE

RICK HUDAK
PM, Meridian Sun #69

Past Master Dale Moritmer and I had a conversation many years ago, and the outcome of it was the opinion that Masonry, for a myriad of reasons, had a major influx of new members after the two World Wars.

For over 200 years, Masonry had attracted many influential, respected, and motivated men who were prepared to take the time to interact with — and learn from — other leaders of their communities, and together practiced the Ancient Craft. Between the millions of young men being sent off to war at the same time and the dismantling of the downtown urban centers for gathering, the numbers of Masons and Masonic Lodges mushroomed. Instead of Lodges being central and urban, it seemed that each crossroads with a name soon had its own Masonic Lodge. Looking back, it almost seems that if a town had a gas station, it had a Masonic Lodge.

Trying to keep this network of real estate viable became a real challenge. And after the peak in the mid 1960s or so, the slow but steady decline in membership seemed to lead to a sort of panic to boost membership.

The next step, in my opinion, was very unfortunate. Becoming a Mason became basically attending a convention. Pay your money, take a day out of your busy life, and call yourself a Mason. Rather than looking back at our heritage and realistically planning, the decision was made to step away from generations of tradition whereby new members were required to prove themselves by learning and returning examinations. This did a number of things, almost none of them good.

This examination process demonstrated to the Lodge — and the candidate in many cases — who had the ability to learn and give back ritual. The one thing that these new standards did, for a while at least, was level off the decline in members (and dues).

We have faced much the same problem as many other organizations and churches. Declining real income and membership; maintaining real estate; and attracting members has consumed much of our time and resources. Our real short-term dilemma here is how to fairly and sensibly consolidate our facilities.

I know that in Meridian Sun Lodge, once we were able to move our focus from figuring out how to pay for our own building, utilities, taxes, etc., and we were able to concentrate on having fun events and being more visible in our community, then we did have a considerable influx of members — the "old fashioned" way of staging three separate degrees. We partnered with our municipality and have insured our financial future for at least the next 20 years. We also have methods in place to be sure that we have the resources to continue well beyond that.

I really do not want to be too critical here, but you did ask the question. I would rather see one sincere, well motivated Mason join my Lodge than ten guys who want to show up for a day, get to wear a ring, and, in a few years, have to be pestered to pay their dues.

I would like to see Masonry remain quality rather than quantity, and if that eventually means 100-200 Lodges in Ohio, then maybe that is the way it is supposed to be.

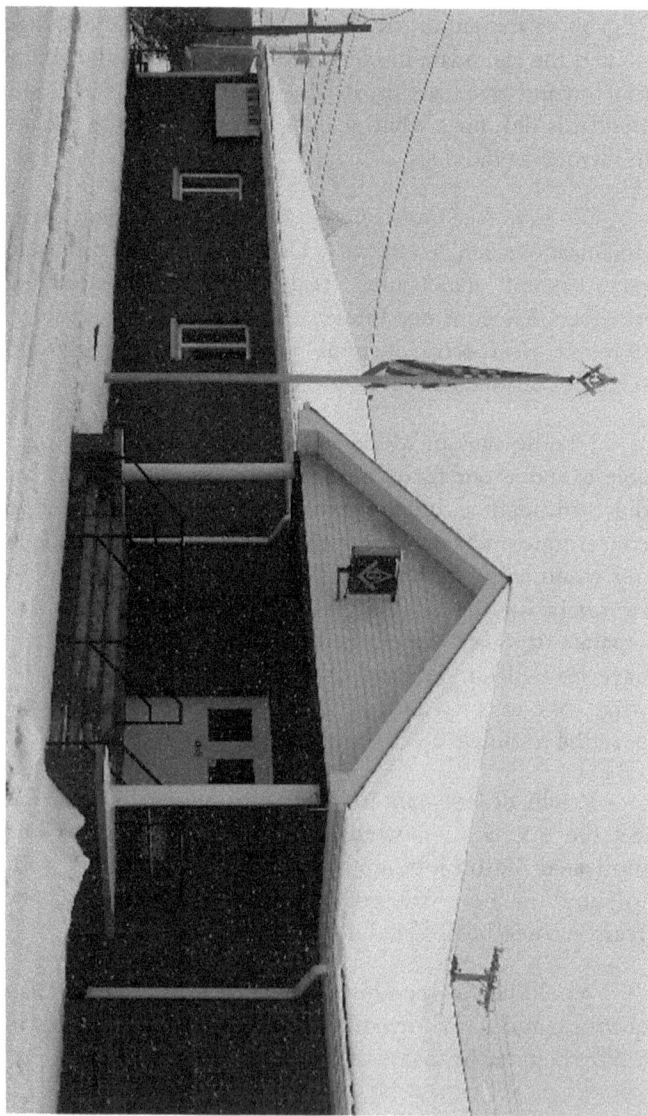

Dennison Temple, February 2015. By Easterling.

THOMAS G. HUTCHINS, SR.
PDDGM/PM, Stow #768

What makes a Lodge successful?

Contrary to a generally held view, it is *not* a large number of members, nor a large bank account, nor large numbers of new members on an annual basis.

I think a successful Lodge has a membership sufficiently uniform to be compatible, yet diverse enough to be interesting.

A successful Lodge will most likely have a sufficient number of its membership who are willing to be involved in the Lodge functions, support Lodge activities, and willing to go the extra mile for the fraternity.

A successful Lodge will have a variety of activities that are of interest to and involve a majority of the membership — as well as the families of the members. Contrary, a Lodge that tries to have activities of interest to *all* of its members is on a fool's journey.

A successful Lodge will have a presence in the community.

A successful Lodge will have a knowledgeable, capable secretary with good communion skills.

A successful Lodge will have a good, functioning communication system to ensure its membership is well informed.

THE SUCCESSFUL LODGE

A successful Lodge will see itself as a member of fraternity, not a local club.

A successful Lodge will most likely have several members that are well known to members of other Lodges in the area.

A successful Lodge will most likely have a few members that visit other Lodges in the area on a regular basis, not just during annual inspections.

What is necessary to have a successful Lodge?

A membership with a sufficient number of the members willing to undertake the responsibility of being a good officer.

A cadre of Past Masters willing to advise — yet *not* control — the officer line.

A knowledgeable, capable secretary with good communication skills.

A membership free of debilitating infighting, factions, and cliques.

Adequate funds to keep the Lodge functioning and paying its bills. This would include dues sufficient to cover daily operational expenses.

Members interested in learning more about the fraternity and visiting other Lodges.

Activities that are of interest to the general membership.

A decent educational program for new members and new officers of the Lodge.

A meeting location that is fairly easy to access, with adequate parking and handicap-accessible.

How do you make a Lodge successful?

I am not sure that you can *make* a Lodge successful.

The members must want their Lodge to be successful, by *their* standards, not some outside metric.

That said, encouraging Lodge members to be involved is always a good place to start

Encourage Lodge members to embrace their Lodge activities and to be supportive of the officers.

Encourage Lodge members to learn about Masonic history while creating their own history.

Ensure Lodge's annual dues are sufficient to cover its cost of operation. And to review its dues every few years, and increase them as necessary, to meets its operational costs.

Encourage Lodge members to visit many other Lodges, thereby increasing the feeling of a viable fraternity, and not just a local club.

Ensure that the Lodge's meeting location is easy to access, with ample parking and handicapped-accessible.

RICHARD JANKURA
SD, Meridian Sun #69

What makes a Lodge successful?

Dedicated, experienced Brethren who care about doing things right. And communicating the deeper meaning behind the ritual.

What is necessary to have a successful Lodge?

Committed line officers and Past Masters that help new line officers to understand what they should be doing. A good secretary and treasurer are also essential.

How do you make a Lodge successful?

I take my responsibilities seriously, and if I commit to do something, I want to do it to the best of my ability. If I cannot, then I need to be able to tell that to the leaders, and they need to be understanding of the same.

ROBERT JERNIGAN
PM, Barberton #750

In your experience, what makes a Lodge successful?

Activities involving families. Also, activities with other Lodges.

What is necessary to have a successful Lodge?

Lodges must do more than just do ritualistic work and practices. They need to have activities that make members want to attend. Get newer members involved in Lodge work (ex. Fellowcraft team, help in preparation room) — any activity that makes them feel like part of the Lodge.

How do you make a Lodge successful?

I don't feel you can make a Lodge successful; we have to find a way to make them *want* their Lodge to be successful. This is the hard part.

EDDIE KEE
PM and WM, William H. Hoover #770

What makes a Lodge successful?

Having a line of non-PMs? Yes!

Having a full Lodge room? Yes!

Having a stream of candidates? Yes!

Having good ritual work? Yes!

Having Masonic Educational Programs? Yes!

Having non-Masonic Education Programs? Yes!

Having fellowship time? Yes!

Having fun? Yes!

Having family activities? Yes!

Having kids around? Yes!

What does it take to make a Lodge successful?

All of these are needed and desirable for a successful Lodge. The problem is how to get there.

Communication is what makes a Lodge successful. Without communication, none of the above will happen.

BEST PRACTICES IN FREEMASONRY

The Brethren need to be part of what is going on in the Lodge, and they need to make it their Lodge.

The hardest problem we have is how to communicate this to the membership. We have text messages, email, web sites, newsletters, and emails — but if there is no personal connection, then the communication fails.

Something that I always keep in the back of my mind harkens back to when I was asking my dad about Masons, and shortly after joining finding out that he had not been to Lodge in fifteen years.

He joined, knew of other members, paid his dues, but he did not go to Lodge. I asked why he stayed away, and he said he was embarrassed for not going in all of those years. And he went on to say that if someone had called or stopped out and asked him to attend, then he would have gone.

This method of communication takes the most time, but I have offered to accompany Brothers to Lodge meetings when they had not planned to attend, both in my Lodge and others. This is the most important method of communication that works. And it is the hardest. It is like being a salesman who has to experience many doors slammed in his face. However, once it works, then the other methods of communication will continue to work.

So what makes a good Lodge? Communication. And the rest is easy.

THE SUCCESSFUL LODGE

What will I do to make this happen?

The same thing I did in 2001-2002: Start calling and inviting the Brothers out. And hopefully the other officers will do the same. Gather email addresses for all of the Brothers. Foster dialog with the Star and Job's daughters.

We can and do change our activities throughout the year, based on the desire of the members. In the past year, I found out that many of the members want to go somewhere after Lodge, and not have refreshment downstairs. The Brothers say they want to talk, relax and get to know each other.

This year, William H. Hoover Lodge merged with Julliard Lodge, which was chartered in 1870. Now we have two Lodges operating simultaneously as one Lodge. If I can accomplish the true melding of two Lodges this year, then I will feel like something has been accomplished. It is great to have some fresh perspectives in the Lodge, but getting the members from Julliard to speak up can be a small challenge. Both sides need to realize that they are more than permanent visitors; they now live here.

Some other things will be getting the Lodge to support and help the other two bodies within our Temple.

I was sad when I attended the not-yet-Thanksgiving dinner that the girls had, and there were only about 10 people there. It was very well publicized within the Order of the Eastern Star and the Lodge, but attendance was lacking. When I do not go to special events like this, it is usually not due to some other activity with my family; it is usually due to a lack of connection. And being in the same building is not enough connection. I will invite the Job's Daughters and OES to our meeting, and not to just serve dinner, but to share in some of our programs.

BEST PRACTICES IN FREEMASONRY

Earlier this fall, I approached a young lady who will be graduating from college and asked her to help with our church's stewardship campaign. As the head of finance committee, I felt that the congregation has heard enough from me about the church's finances. This young lady said she would be involved, but with one condition: NO MEETINGS. She said that they are not productive, and everything can be said in a ten-minute phone call.

This is also why our young members lose interest in Lodge. Many times our meeting have become about the opening, minutes, bills, and closing. If there are not candidates, then we need to make meeting about interest, hobbies, education, and programs.

I had programs the last time I was master, but the programs are still only a small fraction of a meeting. Some programs involve non-Masons, and while there are ways to include them, none are too convenient. It is hard and rude to invite someone to a meeting to make a presentation, then have them wait outside while we open and close a Lodge meeting. It would be helpful if we would have a public opening/closing that could be done in such instances. The business of the Lodge can be done in a brief and efficient business meeting open to the members.

In closing, I feel communication makes the organization function; candidates make the organization grow; programs enlighten the members; fellowship strengthens and binds the members together; and success will ensue.

Dover Temple, February 2015. Photo by Easterling.

JASON KIDD
PM and WM, Mount Akra #680

What makes a Lodge successful?

A successful Lodge is one that is actively involved in the activities of its Masonic district, and in communicating with its Lodge members. When Masons are actively involved in its district, the information can be communicated at Lodge meetings and in bulletins sent to members.

What is necessary to have a successful Lodge?

A Lodge must continue to use all methods to effectively communicate to membership: phone, email, and postal service.

The Lodge must also have line officers that are actively involved in the degree work, education, and activities at the Lodge.

The officers must also have the support of its Past Masters, as this can impact Lodge activities and the perception of some of the older members, who may not attend meetings but communicate with the PMs.

How do you make a Lodge successful?

You make the Lodge successful by learning that change and adaptability can be a good thing sometimes. But also understanding tradition. Keep in mind some of these traditions have made the Lodge what it is today. If you have activities or events that have worked in the past, continue to do those.

Talk to other Lodges who are having success in membership, who get a good turnout at their events.

Speaking with members who are at the stated meetings is also instrumental in determining the pulse of the Lodge.

Bringing in guest speakers is one way to break up the monotony of the stated meeting when members say the reason they don't come is because meetings are boring.

LAWRENCE (LARRY) L. LANDALS
DEO/PM, Summit #213; National #568

I could wrap it up a successful Lodge into one word: FUN.

The stresses of officers to learn their respective stations — as well as memorizing lectures, charges and other parts — the Lodge needs to temper it with relaxing and fun events. There are several facets of a Lodge that bring in new members, as well as bringing old members back to meetings.

One is the impression the officers make on a new candidate with well executed degree work. The candidate will not know the exact wording that is expected to be delivered, but the officer/Brother must be able to give it without several prompts. It takes away from the ceremony when the presenter has to be given several prompts to finish his part. I would rather see a Brother skip a whole paragraph of a lecture that to be prompted through the whole thing.

Two, a Lodge needs to have scheduled events outside of the degree work. After a Brother observes 20-30 degrees, if they are just sitting on the side, it becomes boring to them. If a Lodge has other events, and involves the family on a monthly schedule, then the Brethren have something to share with the fraternity, and they have not simply "gone to Lodge." You can also get the Brothers that are not officers to take charge of these events. That way, they are able to give something back to the Lodge.

To make this all successful, the master should have a full year's calendar of events scheduled, and publish it for the members. It demonstrates the ability of the master to be organized, plus it gives the Brothers events to look forward to. The events need to be geared to the whole family, as well as to their significant other. Twice a year, we offer a ladies' night out, where the Brethren can take their significant other out to dinner, and maybe dancing or a show. This decreases the secrecy of the fraternity for the women, and it allows us to show our personalities to everyone.

To sum this all up: having FUN, a well scheduled Lodge, and proficient officers create success.

I could go on with other things that make a Lodge successful. As a write this, the flood gates open up with so many specifics that create success. To be short, another is the involvement of new and older members. The master and officers should be involving members that are not officers, so they have a sense of pride that they are giving back to the Lodge. Maybe they have a charity that has meaning to them, that the Lodge could support.

RICHARD LANDALS
DDGM/PM, National #568

What makes a Lodge successful?

In my experience, a Lodge has multiple "success" levels, which are measured by membership and retention of its members, activities, and programs within the Lodge, officer leadership, and ritual proficiency. While each sector may see triumphs, all areas must work together in order to have a successful Lodge.

What is necessary to have a successful Lodge?

A Lodge cannot support itself unless the membership energetically supports the programs and activities within the organization. When these goals are met, members actively pursue acceptance within the Lodge, all while promoting the fraternity to others.

Once embedded into the Lodge, members are eager to lead and take active roles within the management of the Lodge, leading others and growing the membership base. With pride and accomplishment as a passenger, proficiency in the ritual work becomes a natural fit. The culmination of these junctures are essential for a Lodge to be successful.

How do you make a Lodge successful?

One tool in providing Lodge success is centered on meeting the needs of its members.

THE SUCCESSFUL LODGE

A membership interest survey can highlight areas and provide an analysis of membership goals and interests. Analyze and nurture these goals. And promote new ones once they are met, being careful not to overload its members and the roles they play.

Another tool the Lodge can use: facilitate teamwork and leadership development programs, utilizing online training courses and regional workshops. Recognize their comfort level, and do not coerce them into roles for which they will fail. An empowered leader is attuned to the roles of the Lodge and its membership.

Each Lodge can also utilize tools provided by its Grand Lodge. Ohio offers a typewritten ritual, which is one example, and is available for each Lodge to use. It provides in-depth knowledge about the ritualistic work of each degree. It also aids in understanding the floor work; which may have been miscommunicated or "lost" over the years when members retire from the Lodge.

While each tool can stand on its own, the culmination of these items enable the Lodge to be successful!

DAVID J. LANNI
PM, Mount Akra #680

What makes a Lodge successful?

Lodges are successful if they have a good core of Officers and they work together as a team. They also need to call their members occasionally and try to get them to come out.

What is necessary to have a successful Lodge?

To have a successful Lodge you need the above as well as a good selection of out-of-Lodge functions for family participation.

How do you make a Lodge successful?

In order for me to make a successful Lodge I would make sure we have a calling committee which we always had. I think it is very important to keep in contact with your members. I have not received a call from my Lodge since 1998 when I was Master for my 3rd time. I would also make sure anyone who wanted to help would be given something to do.

MICHAEL LENGLER
DDGM/PM, Tuscarawas #59

In my experience, the secret to a successful Lodge begins with leadership. The Worshipful Master has the most responsibility and should prepare for his year in the East. The Master of the Lodge should lead by example. He needs to display good ritual work and expect the same from his subordinate officers. If he leads by example, he will command respect, rather than demanding respect. The Master should also have an attentive ear and instructive tongue. It takes wisdom, and it takes good communication with the other officers of the Lodge.

If the above is achieved, all else should fall in place.

The next step is for a member of the Lodge to plant a seed, and it will grow. Harmony is the strength and support of all institutions, especially this.

JOSEPH LEVY
PDDGM/Secretary, Ashlar #639

What makes a Lodge successful?

1. A solid core of members and officers willing to accept responsibility and carry forth assigned duties and responsibilities assigned to them.

2. A steady influx of new petitions.

3. Degree work presented according to the ritual. Practice and exemplification brings proficiency.

4. High level of self-esteem that comes from knowledge and proficiency.

5. Financial security.

6. Inspiration, convenience, enthusiasm.

7. Truly caring for one another before looking to external secular charities to support.

8. Strong ties to a community through some type of civic or social involvement.

9. Focus on specific goals.

10. Meetings that do not last longer than necessary. Realize that everyone's time is valuable.

THE SUCCESSFUL LODGE

What is necessary to have a successful Lodge?

1. A core of senior members who are willing to mentor the newer members in the history of the Lodge and the ways of the fraternity.

2. Innovative Lodge education programs that touch upon all of the above.

3. Minimize negative criticism. Promote critical thinking and positive mentoring that raises self-esteem.

4. Do not be afraid to spend some money — within means — on the membership. It can pay dividends.

5. Good communication, not only between the master and the members, but between the members in general.

6. Sharing ideas. Do not be afraid to try new things, as long as the new ideas are consistent with our rules and constitutions.

7. Family involvement. Wives and children have to buy in and participate.

8. Do not hesitate to explain to your wife and children why it is important for you to be a member and participate.

9. Value members' time. Do not squander or waste it with meaningless meetings that are held just for the sake of having a meeting.

10. Know and live our rules and ways. Make sure that your actions scream so loud that people do not need to hear what you are saying.

BEST PRACTICES IN FREEMASONRY

How do you make a Lodge successful?

1. Change can be good — as long we are not compromising our own rules and constitutions. Be innovative. Think out of the box.

2. Mentor rather than complain.

3. Be a fraternity of caring communicators.

4. Honor our core values.

5. Write down long- and short-term goals, and continuously re-evaluate their progress.

6. Have a written agenda to maximize time efficiency.

7. Be fiscally responsible, but not overly cautious.

8. Continue to promote the value of having new members come into the Lodge — along with the opportunities that they may present.

9. Share ideas and experiences among members.

10. All members need to understand that there is no advancement by entitlement in Masonry; only advancement through knowledge and proficiency.

11. Numbers are not the goal. If we are really good at focusing on our core values, then the numbers will take care of themselves.

12. Finally, an individual cannot make a Lodge successful; only by its members, working together through effective leadership, and focused goal achievement, can a Lodge become successful.

Gnadenhutten Temple, February 2015.
Photo by Easterling.

BILL LOVELL
SD, Wayfarer #789

What makes a Lodge successful?

I do not have a lot of experience in Freemasonry, but since I was raised in the Spring of 2013, I have seen that the Lodge improves dramatically when we interact with newer Brothers and Brothers that visit less often.

What is necessary to have a successful Lodge?

It is imperative that we do not form cliques, and that we spend our time in refreshment with Lodge members we do not already know well. We need to stand near them, sit with them, and talk with them whenever we get a chance. They do not know the ways of the Lodge, and they feel like outsiders before they even come in. We need to show our spirit of Brotherhood from the very start.

How do you make a Lodge successful?

Encourage the officers to take the lead in including the newer Brothers, and in contacting the Brothers who do not attend as often. We need to ask them to help and to join in the work we do. If they have a constructive part, they are more apt to stick around and encourage others to do the same.

BOB MARTELET
PM, William McKinley #431

What makes a Lodge successful?

Commitment!

What is necessary to have a successful Lodge?

Planning!

How do you make a successful Lodge?

Attendance!

Now let me expand. I wrote an editorial on attendance in the September, 2014 issue of the *Masonic Bulletin*. That article generated some interesting comments, and I am not finished with that controversy yet.

I was asked, while I was master of my Lodge many years ago, to present a fifty-year pin to a Brother of our Lodge.

Only thing was: I was to present this award to him in a neighboring Lodge, rather than in his own.

After the presentation — grand honors and all — during the quiet period after the hurrah, being young and inquisitive, I asked this old Mason why he did not attend his home Lodge any longer.

He exclaimed, "After you have been a member as long as me, I hope you do not become disillusioned, as I am."

I figured he was a stubborn old fogy, and I went on with my life.

Now that attendance is such a large problem with Masonic Lodges today, I wonder if his statement was the beginning of the future. I mean to say: With the average age of Masons being 65+ years, and with many a Brother stating that Lodge is "boring," do they actually mean they are disillusioned?

What makes a Lodge successful?

When I was appointed to the line, which in those days was a ten year trip, there were six other fellows who were also eligible for that honor. In those days, you had better show you were committed, or you would be passed over.

When in a station, you should know the next station, and be ready to execute it at any time.

The same goes with memory work. When the junior warden assumes the west, his memory work should be completed, which will give him time for planning.

The master should be able to assume any lecture or charge if the case arrives. He is the master of the Lodge. A ship's master can start the engines if the engineer is out of commission! The Brethren on the sidelines want a leader who can take over and lead. The Master does not follow; he knows and he leads. He plans. He executes.

What makes a Lodge successful?

The new Master should announce his plans and calendar of events for his whole year the night of his installation.

THE SUCCESSFUL LODGE

People are very busy, short of money sometimes, and need months to plan a big event to attend.

If you announce a short Lodge trip a month before the bus leaves, the event is doomed before it gets off the ground.

The youth need to get their heads out of their butts, take their noses out of their cell phones, and think. Planning is what makes projects successful. Milisecond around-the-world communication is great, but it will never be the same as the time you spend together during that date circled on the family calendar.

How do you make a Lodge successful?

A successful Lodge has lots of Brethren on the sidelines, all contributing to the meeting. It's their Lodge, so why shouldn't they contribute? Each Brother has something of importance to add.

They also like to learn. Speakers on outside subjects are great, and each officer should supply a program or subject for discussion at some time each year. I am close to 70 years now. I can't see great any longer. Hearing is starting to go away. Attention span is questionable. But I am not bored in Lodge. Disillusioned? Maybe! But still very interested in what the Lodge has to get accomplished.

I once talked to a Past Master who saw it necessary to guide his Lodge in surrendering a 100 year old charter. I'm sure he thought he was correct. He does not talk to me much today, because of what I said when I was talking with him after the event.

My statement was simply, "Good thing I was not a member of your Lodge. You would have had to fight me every inch of the way and maybe even in the parking lot before I would have let that Charter go!"

He acted like giving up 100 years of history was of no bigger deal than closing a second-rate novel before going to sleep. Here again: no real commitment.

THE SUCCESSFUL LODGE

BILL McCALLUM
<u>PM, Ashlar #639</u>

What makes a successful Lodge?

Participation. No Lodge can survive without the membership getting involved. Brethren must be interested in the ritual that has to be done. And they must help each other achieve proficiency. (That is the purpose of the Blue Lodge.)

What is necessary to have a successful Lodge?

Selection is a big thing and we should look at all candidates, as to why they want to join. We have embarked on a mission to make Lodges as big as possible and given up on our beginnings. We no longer need to know a candidate for any length of time, therefore we know very little about him. We have taken the mystery out of the process. Whether we like it or not, we are now soliciting for members.

How do you make a Lodge successful?

I rest my case. Selection and participation is the basis for success. If we select the right candidates and we get participation, we achieve success. I don't know what is meant by a successful Lodge other than men coming together and setting examples on how to become better men. I don't think a successful Lodge means money, numbers of members, or how many charities we contribute to, only in the case of helping each other, when in need, which is what we are supposed to do.

RAY McCLELLAND, JR.
WM, Caldwell #330

What makes a Lodge successful?

People make a Lodge successful.

Dedicated members who allow the Lodge to meet several criteria:

One is that the Lodge accepts the right members and puts on good degree work.

Two, that the Lodge is active as financially possible in the community.

Three, educating their members about Masonry, as well as what it takes to improve themselves as men, thus making good men better.

Four, facilitate an environment of Brotherly Love among all members.

What is necessary to have a successful Lodge?

A Worshipful Master who is a facilitator rather than a dictator.

A core of officers and members who are supportive and well versed in Masonry. A Lodge as a whole must be filled with men who are focused together to reach the same common goal.

THE SUCCESSFUL LODGE

How do you make a Lodge successful?

Each member has different roles in the Lodge. With that being said, all must contribute their part to make a Lodge successful.

I make the Lodge a success by doing my part and never settling for just getting by, striving to make my Lodge the best Blue Lodge.

As the Worshipful Master, I must facilitate changes where needed, and keep everyone on the same page and striving in the same direction.

The integrity of the fraternity must always be my number one priority.

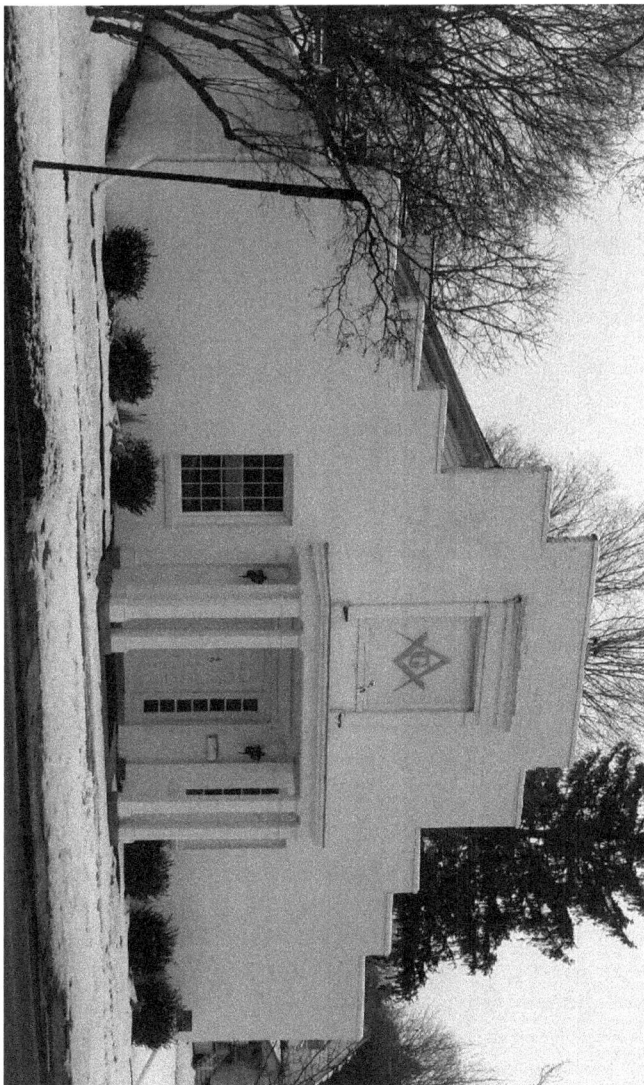

Hudson Temple, January 2015. Photo by Easterling.

RICK MILLER
DEO/PM, William H. Hoover #770

To answer the question, one must first define success. Synonyms of successful are: acknowledged, extraordinary, champion, flourishing, crowned, the best, etc. And one must be able to measure the success in some manner.

Some Lodges may say that the number of members on the role may determine if a Lodge is successful.

Others may say that having sufficient finances makes a Lodge successful.

And others may count the number of members that have filled Grand Lodge positions of responsibility makes a Lodge successful.

While all these aspects are important, I think a Lodge is successful when the members of that Lodge *want* to come to meetings and be involved in the functions the Lodge provides.

Leadership and communication go a long way in determining what Lodge members want. And then organize and communicate with the members to keep them well informed. When members have confidence in their leadership, they are willing to support their leaders, and things happen in a positive way. To bring this about, you have to attain leaders who are willing to learn and willing to lead.

Too many times, we have leaders that are in positions to lead *only* because no one else is willing to do the job.

We also have leaders who become one-man armies because no one is willing to support, follow, and work alongside the leader, maybe due to personality conflicts or some other personal issue.

Regardless, having the right people in the right position at the right time can make all the difference in the world as to what happens in a Lodge.

Bottom line: To be successful, a Lodge needs well informed and organized leaders who want to lead and know how to lead. And then each Lodge and master must determine, year by year, what is most important to that Lodge for that time period. And that takes constant review, constant communication, and constant dedication.

THOMAS MILLER
LEO & SD, Tubal #551

What makes a Lodge successful?

Developing your new members as soon as they come through the door; never give them a chance to lose interest.

See that they are provided with some Lodge responsibility, starting with the Fellowcraft Team. Don't throw them in a chair before they are ready.

What is necessary to have a successful Lodge?

Good programing.

Supporting the Worshipful Master.

Lodge involvement in the Community.

How do you make a Lodge successful?

It takes a village to make a Lodge successful. No one Brother can make a Lodge successful. It starts with successful and nurturing mentoring.

STEVE MOROSKO
PM, Canton #60

A Lodge is a success if it serves its members.

To have a successful Lodge, you need motivated, positive-thinking, enthusiastic, active officers and members.

Its membership needs to be stable or moderately growing. And it needs to have a balanced budget.

It needs to offer some value to its members. Everyone who enters the Lodge should feel welcomed.

To make it even better, each part of each degree, funeral etc. should have at least two active members that can do that part.

The Lodge should have an active website and an active Facebook account. Active meaning they are updated at least monthly.

All event dates should be posted online.

There should be events open to the public to promote new membership.

All members should be contacted at least once a year (and not just to pay dues, but to see how they are doing).

You make a successful Lodge by helping out where you can and when you can. Even the smallest act by each person can combine into a monumental effort as a group.

The Successful Lodge

ERIC MUEHLENBEIN
<u>SW, Canton #60</u>

What makes a Lodge successful?

The success of a Lodge is solely in the hands of the membership. The Worshipful Master and his officers are there to guide and instruct.

Members who embrace Masonry and think about the lessons learned on a daily basis will practice those teachings, to the point where it is no longer something that they need to think about doing, and it becomes automatic.

A Master that keeps things interesting and engaging will hopefully reflect back with increased attendance and interaction by the members.

Ultimately, the success of a Lodge is achieved one Mason at a time, building upon themselves and each other.

What is necessary to have a successful Lodge?

Excitement, enthusiasm, and very importantly, youth.

When the average age of membership is in the 60's, we need to make things more attractive to the younger generation, who will be our successors. We cannot forget the older membership and what they contribute or have contributed in the past, either.

A blend of the two in the form of excitement can be a challenge, but is not impossible. We must keep an open mind to the younger generation that may look, or do things differently. The same goes for the older generation, and for the same reasons.

Remember: It is the internal, and not the external. And we are all striving to be better men.

When I see a new petitioner come in, and I see their enthusiasm, I think about the enthusiasm that I have, and I try to feed theirs to keep it strong. In the same light, engaging the older members can rekindle their enthusiasm.

How do you make a Lodge successful?

Lead by example. How can I ask someone to do something that I cannot do myself?

I tend to jump right in to many things, learn as much as I can, and to ask questions when I don't know the answer. My hope is that by doing so, it inspires others to do the same. I have satisfaction knowing that if I can pass something on, and they, in turn, pass it on to another, I am serving my Brethren well.

THE SUCCESSFUL LODGE

WILLIAM E. MURPHY
DDGM/PM, Stow #768

At its most basic, I think that a Masonic Lodge is a three-legged stool: It is a group of people that...

1. enjoy one another's company,

2. hold a general common belief system (or ritual), and

3. have a good time together.

If any of these legs are pulled out, then the stool falls, and you have problems.

This means that a Lodge needs:

1. people to get together regularly (for social interaction. If they stop attending there are problems.)

2. a common ritual to reinforce our belief system. (If we lose our ritual, or it is poorly handled, you again have problems.)

3. social and charitable activities that people find interesting and useful (to have a good time)

You need leadership to make this happen. This leadership needs to understand our common traditions and be able to think outside the box, to identify activities to appeal to a changing membership.

In addition, the leaders of the Lodge need to ensure that the Lodge is financially prosperous.

The Master cannot handle this alone. He needs to consider working with all interested members and follow a planning process to:

1. set goals and objectives (both short and long term) related to activities, ritual, financial, etc.

2. identify alternative courses of actions to reach these goals

3. choose an alternative based on the stated goals and objectives

4. and finally, develop an action plan.

I do not think "one plan fits all," either for all Lodges or for one individual Lodge. As a result, periodically following a planning process is important for a Lodge to be successful.

Kenmore Temple, January 2015. By Easterling.

NATHAN B. MUTSCHELKNAUS
WM, Tuscarawas #59

These are several questions I have pondered myself over the years. Recently, I started considering things a little differently and began collecting feedback from others. I have now been a quality specialist and data analyst for the government for the past several years. I started wondering, "What would I be doing differently if I treated the Lodge more as a business and its members as our customers?"

Surprisingly, I found out not much would change. EXCEPT: I would want to find out what the customer requirements are. What are their expectations?

The question you *always* ask is: What do people value?

What makes a Lodge successful?

The first thing to consider is: What do the members of your Lodge value and how present is it?

If the members of your Lodge value good degree work, and you rarely confer degrees, they might find the Lodge to be lacking the thing they desire.

It's a good idea to get feedback from both those that attend and those that do not attend, to find out the reasons for both.

You may even find a common theme among those attending and those not attending, regarding what they value and would like to see more present in the future.

A recent example of this is a common theme of all members valuing their family and time with them. This would lead to a recommendation for the Lodge to offer more family-friendly activities and gatherings.

The Successful Lodge

What is necessary to have a successful Lodge?

ENGAGEMENT.

There's no more basic of an answer than this.

You can bring in as many new candidates as you want, or have the largest number of members. However, if you are not engaging the new members, bringing them in and making them feel valued, it won't be long until they just become another card-carrying member.

More importantly, it's critical that you get in touch with some of those members who have not been engaged for a while and find out why.

Nothing is more important than seeing a Lodge with membership participation on the rise. It speaks volumes as to whether you are truly listening to your members and securing a good environment for growth and sustainability. A lot of times, when members are not engaged, it becomes harder and harder to bring in new candidates, as well as get current members that are participating motivated.

We discovered that some of our members are not attending because they are not able, or feel they should not drive at night. Knowing that, we have planned to try and find out how big this need actually is right now. What we have done about it today is simply make some calls to some of the Brethren and offer them rides to and from our stated Lodge meetings.

How do you make a Lodge successful?

You do whatever it takes.

Knowing is half the battle. Knowing what people want. Knowing what people need. Ask questions and get feedback. As a basic rule of thumb, people feel more valued when they feel like you listened to them.

Part of being successful is also about being honest. Honest about the steps that we can take to make things better tomorrow than they were today. And being honest about when those things are going to take some time.

Along with a promise to be honest, we must make a promise to act. To act on the things that we hear, and not just take them into consideration. Being honest and acting on feedback really leads to building trusting relationships with the members of your Lodge. We're all in this together, and while we might have different ideas about how to go about doing things, it really comes down to this: we all want what's best for our beloved Fraternity.

A general comment: Examining quality work, we've found that people often tend to leave the most feedback when they are not pleased about their experience.

People usually do not provide feedback, or provide little feedback, when something happens that was expected — nothing out of the ordinary. However, you know you nailed it when people's feedback tells a story. Something happened that was unexpected. A pleasant surprise, if you will... Those are the moments that people cherish. Everyone wants to have a story to tell. Good or bad. It's just about setting up the right conditions for something unique and memorable.

MARK OHLINGER
Brother, Star #187

What makes a Lodge successful?

Having members that want to be at Lodge, who want to learn and talk about what they have learned, and about how they can apply what they have learned in their lives.

What is necessary to have a successful Lodge?

Having a Lodge that has a warm, open, and inviting atmosphere, where members want to teach and learn from one another.

How do you make a Lodge successful?

I think having a successful Lodge requires a strong leadership team that would first generate a vision of what a successful Lodge would look like. The team would then have a plan to implement to achieve that vision by engaging and directing their members who would be working towards the vision.

JESSE RAY PERTEE
JW, Wadsworth #385

What makes a Lodge successful?

Engage in fellowship outside of the Lodge. Have meaningful meetings not just read bills and minutes.

Be exciting. Engage with the community, make people want to be a part of something bigger than themselves.

What is necessary to have a successful Lodge?

Leadership that is well grounded in Masonic values but not afraid to try new things.

How do you make a Lodge successful?

I engage the community. Facebook, parades, community activities such as relay for life, and the blue tip. Men see us and what we are doing and want to be a part of something special.

STANTON PHELPS
<u>PM, Coventry-Akron #83</u>

What makes a Lodge successful?

An interested membership that attends Lodge because it is an interesting place to be, as well as providing fellowship and good company in general.

What is necessary to have a successful Lodge?

An interesting program for each meeting (especially so for stated meetings and degree work). Keeping the Brethren's attention. And providing an atmosphere that invites participation.

How do you make a Lodge successful?

It takes a lot of work from the line officers, the trustees, and a whole lot of "good vibrations" from the regular participants.

Who wants to come to Lodge and listen to people complain about a "lack of funding" or "insufficient income"? We should be planning some sort of fundraising projects to alleviate the situation, not running down the very people who are trying to get something new started.

Minerva Temple, January 2015. Photo by Easterling.

THE SUCCESSFUL LODGE

D. MITCH REARICK
Brother, Coventry-Akron #83

What makes a Lodge successful?

I feel it is having committed, active members.

What is necessary to have a successful Lodge?

I feel it is having committed, active members.

How do you make a Lodge successful?

Unfortunately, I do not follow my own feelings on this. I have not attended Lodge for quite some time due to family and business commitments. As I approach retirement, I have hoped to become more active.

JERRY REGULA
PM, Port Washington #202

What makes a Lodge successful?

1) A successful Lodge is an active one.

How do we stay active?

Good leadership. Good leaders listen — and actually pay attention to what people are saying.

Good mix of members with varying ages and interests.

Focus towards activities that interest people. Not the approach of saying, "You *have* to do this."

Lead by example, always positive, active.

What is necessary to have a successful Lodge?

See answer #1.

How do you make a Lodge successful?

I do what I can, when I can. I have been traveling for work and unable to make a lot of meetings. I stay in touch and help when I can.

I am the chaplain. I help with steak fries and the French fry stand. We had a member that has unfortunately passed. I believe he was over 80. Up to the time of passing, he still helped with peeling potatoes for steak fries and being a craftsman. He did not know it, but he led by example. Doing what he was able to do. Always positive. We can encourage members to do the same.

You can have a family, work, and take some time to be active. We are taught to divide the hours of the day into three equal parts. This is part of the recipe for a healthy lifestyle which I hope to enjoy until the day I am called home.

DAN RIGGLE
PM, Ebenezer #33

My mind looks at our fraternity and asks questions, so if you'll allow me…

What makes a Lodge successful?

Several things to look at:

Do the officers contribute to activities and take part in the annual program?

Does the Lodge's senior leaders bring the officers along their journey to see and develop good leadership practices?

Can a member come to Lodge and enjoy the proceedings, and not be asked to sit in the seat of an officer? Is there an agenda for the meeting, to keep it on track?

Is the Master aware of the events surrounding the Lodge? And does he keep in contact with the secretary and treasurer?

Can the Lodge stay in contact with the members they don't always see in Lodge?

What is necessary to be a successful Lodge?

Can we discuss our differences and leave the discussion as friends and Brothers?

Can you look forward to going to a Lodge meeting? Can you look back and say, "That was worth the night out"?

THE SUCCESSFUL LODGE

Do the officers look forward to the years to come? Do they plan for several different routes to take, or at least, are they prepared to address issues that come up, and not let challenges fester into disasters?

Does the climate allow change to take place to improve the Lodge? Can the climate be created by leaders of the Lodge?

How do you make a Lodge successful?

Can I see a problem in the simple things that can be brought the attention of the Master (tactfully)?

The simple things tend to make a difference for most all our Brothers:

Can I help?

Can I keep quiet about how things were?

Can I see a Lodge in the future that I want our Lodge to be?

Can I see a mistake that I made in the past that is still being made (perhaps because I did that)?

STEVEN STERTZBACH
<u>WM, Clinton #47</u>

What makes a Lodge successful?

I believe what is first and foremost in making a Lodge successful is strong, knowledgeable, and dedicated leadership.

I am not just talking about the line core officers, although this is an important part of the equation. You need someone that is dedicated to giving their time in guiding the officers and making it an enjoyable experience.

Second, I believe you need to get everyone involved in the Lodge, from asking new members to fill positions when possible, to getting everyone involved in Lodge activities.

What is necessary to have a successful Lodge?

First, the aforementioned leadership. Then I believe you need to have programs and activities that are geared not only to our Brothers, but their families as well.

How do you make a Lodge successful?

By striving to make the officers, as well as the members, knowledgeable about Masonry and what it stands for.

The Successful Lodge

By doing in the individual Lodges what you are doing here: asking the members what they think makes a successful Lodge.

Then try to incorporate their suggestions into the Lodge activities.

Also, by setting reasonable attainable goals both in the individual Lodges and the Grand Lodge. There are times when goals and expectations are set so high that one might have a tendency to shy away from getting involved, because they feel it is taking away from their family life, or — just as importantly — their spouse feels it is too time consuming and taking away from family time. As I said before, it needs to be an enjoyable experience for all.

RICK STEWARD
LEO, Conrad #271

What makes a Lodge successful?

Strong leadership of the Lodge Officers.

And interesting meetings.

What is necessary to have a successful Lodge?

An excited and interested membership.

How do you make a Lodge successful?

Try and make the Lodge Education program as interesting as possible, by bringing in speakers and promoting an exciting education program this year.

I am personally excited for this Masonic year, and I express that feeling with members of Conrad Lodge and other Lodges. I hope my enthusiasm will be contagious.

North Canton Temple, January 2015. By Easterling.

BILL STRATTON
PDDGM/PM, Charity #530

What makes a Lodge successful?

All the Brethren thinking the same, and working together to make it a success.

What is necessary to have a successful Lodge?

Informing all your members what is happening, and asking their opinions on all things that need to be done.

How do you make a Lodge successful?

Keep the members informed, work with all the officers, have a number of events for the entire family. Consider all the opinions given to you. Work together!

THE SUCCESSFUL LODGE

KEVIN TANNER
DEO/PM, Adoniram-Joppa #517

The foundation of a successful Lodge is certainly Lodge leadership.

The essence of a successful Lodge is relationships.

There are many instances in our Masonic lessons that allude to the importance of relationships; our duty to our neighbor; Brotherly love, relief and truth; contributing to the relief of worthy distressed Master Masons; the cement which unites us into a society of friends and Brothers; the list goes on.

But without a fraternal bond of friendship, there is no reason for a Brother to even come to Lodge, let alone be active. Each of us can name someone who is — or was — an inspiration to us. We must be diligent in communicating with our Brethren and caring for them as part of our duty as Masons.

ROY TURNER
PM, Adoniram-Joppa #517

As a Lodge, we must impress the candidate from the start with:

- Good attendance by all members

- Good ritual work

- Quality in our selection of officers

- Guidelines, duties, and ritual goals for officers at all stations

- Interesting training programs, like T.E.L.L., Series IV-V

- Commitment and example set by top officers

- Service and Assistance to our Brethren

Every new and veteran member has to maintain that feeling from the heart, that obligation to attend and support his Lodge. He needs to be ever impressed by good ritual work, the very best that an officer can give. When he sees excellent work, he will want to get involved himself.

The Lodge should be particularly careful to select men who will be eager to serve the officer line, who should be willing to take courses on the Grand Lodge Handbook and leadership. They should work with mentors on lectures and charges and movement, to the end that they know the floor work well. Study hard, study well.

Younger officers should have a guideline chart of their ritual progress, and they should keep current. This all falls under commitment from the heart, that you learn well, so that you may teach and impress others. Make them proud of the Lodge they joined, whether or not they become an officer.

A key to successful Lodges is having an officer corps that works together as a tight-knit team to make the Lodge experience for members significant and enjoyable. This begins with the welcoming hand of fellowship and continues with dignified degree work and fun social events.

An effort or message needs to come from the heart of the master, to the hearts of his members to return to Lodge; to fill those seats on degree night to the benefit of the Candidate. Go the extra mile to fill the seats on nights of inspections and represent his Lodge; to fill the seats at dinner tables and share in the fellowship; to fill his own heart and conscience with Truth, for the benefit of his family, workplace and community.

This was my experience upon joining, and I was very impressed. I also learned that Masons look after each other, their widows and orphans. And I have also been witness to these examples of service to one another. Maybe this heartfelt Brotherly Love and assistance is what many Brethren seek today, as it once was from the beginning, before we put emphasis on ritual. The two, together, should be equally promoted and demonstrated among our circle and the community at large.

My advice pales in comparison to the already perfectly written charges, obligations, and lessons that we learn from the encyclopedia of Freemasonry, all of which should apply to our lives.

The lessons are there — we just have to put them to practice, from the heart... then shall we be successful.

JOSEPH B. VILHOSKY
PM, Carol F. Clapp #655, Ohio's 25th
<u>Masonic District; current member of Clinton #47</u>

How do you make a Lodge successful?

A successful Lodge doesn't just happen; it must be planned, just as a successful business is planned.

As the master of your Lodge, meet with all your officers to lay out a five-year plan. The plan must have specific goals for attendance and membership, with detailed programs to put in place. There is not a successful business that I'm aware of that does not have a business plan.

Success does not *happen*; it is planned. Next year, the new master does the same thing with his core of officers and every year thereafter.

If the Lodge does not have an officer or Past Master who has a business background to assist in designing a five-year plan, I recommend they consider contacting their district education officer to see if he, or possibly the Grand Lodge of Ohio, knows of a leadership development program that is reasonable to become active in.

It goes without saying: no program or training will be successful unless the Masons who are at the top in the Lodge are convinced that a program is needed and can be successful.

You don't necessarily need a majority to believe change is needed and the program will work. You just need one person. This one person can be the mechanism to motivate others to assess and take part in the programs.

However, in order for this to occur year after year, it is your duty, as the master of your Lodge, to appoint future officers who want to be informed, are enthusiastic, and dedicated to perform their duties — not only in learning lectures, charges, and degree work, but also being active in the functions of your Lodge.

Yes, when one is appointed or elected into the Masonic line as an officer, it is a great honor. But beyond that, the man must understand, before accepting the responsibility: It is not only for the current year, but for the years thereafter.

You have all heard, "if it's to be, it's up to me." It starts with how proficiently and how conscientiously we do our degree work. Whether Masonry has an important and lasting effect to a Mason starts in the E.A. degree: We should be exact in our ritualistic work, to guarantee that he receives only the best. Flippancy, whispering, and laughing should not be accepted. The candidate comes this way only one time, and he should see and hear the best work that we can give him.

Do you attend and participate in Masonic memorial services?

Do you make a special effort to encourage as many members to attend as possible?

This advice may end up sounding like a laundry list, but it does not exist in isolation. Rather, they form interrelated networks of factors, contained in five personal areas: The use of mental ability, personal characteristics, administrative skills, relations outside Masonry, and the ability to put it all together.

BEST PRACTICES IN FREEMASONRY

Buying and reading this book is your first step in success. You were once told, "Seek and you shall find; knock, and it shall be opened unto you." If you truly want to be successful, and you want your Lodge to be successful, then your next step is to continue seeking and knocking.

Start with your L.E.O. Ask him what courses your Grand Lodge has available, then take them. Sign up for Freemason University and complete their courses. Contact the district education officer and ask how to get into the Grand Lodge Leadership Program. The Grand Lodge is there to help. All you need to do is ask, the same as you would do if you're thirsty or hungry — they will give you drink and food.

The tools to make your Lodge successful are there for you to use. And best of all, the only cost is a little of your time.

New Philadelphia Temple, February 2015.
Photo by Easterling.

BRENNAN WALLICK
DEO/PM, Cypress #604

What makes a Lodge successful?

A core of Past Masters who are willing to help, listen, advise, and allow the master to lead to the best of his ability.

What is necessary to have a successful Lodge?

A group of Brothers who are willing help one another with degree work (Brotherly Love), help one another in and out of Lodge (Relief), and stand beside one another when the tough decisions have to be made (Truth).

How do you make a Lodge successful?

It takes a willingness from all the Brothers of the Lodge to respect one another, participate in any way they can, and being able to enjoy the work they do.

THE SUCCESSFUL LODGE

STEVE WARREN
PM, William H. Hoover #770

What makes a Lodge successful?

The men in the Lodge determine if it is successful. If they are active and participate — not just in the Degree work, but in building the Lodge by mentoring new Masons, making sure all are welcome and feel that they are part of the Lodge & fraternity (including their wives and family) — then the Lodge will grow and be successful. The ritual is important, but if you don't have candidates or enough Masons available to confer the Degrees, the Lodge cannot succeed and grow.

What is necessary to have a successful Lodge?

Good Masons.

Men who are willing to step into leadership roles when asked. Men who are willing to do more than just wear a ring outside of the Lodge.

We like to tell people we "make good men better." To be successful, we need to mentor our new members, keep them engaged in Masonry, and give them a chance to grow in our Fraternity.

Raising a Brother, then sitting him on the sideline is not a good way to grow your Lodge or make it successful. Men who feel, share and live the Brotherhood of our fraternity are the men who come back, participate, and make your Lodge strong.

How do you make a Lodge successful?

After I was raised, I spent six months sitting on the sidelines. I did not feel included, did not have any sense of "Brotherhood." I came close to being a member who only paid dues and wore his ring, while never attending meetings or functions. The very day I was asking myself if I really wanted to keep coming to the meetings, someone suggested to the incoming master that I might make a good officer.

Only after being appointed to the line did I really feel a sense of *belonging* to the Lodge. As I worked through the chairs and had a chance to join and participate in other Masonic organizations, I realized that I needed to be that person who reached out to other Masons — new Brothers and those who only showed up occasionally — to make them feel welcome, wanted, and needed.

Some of the masters who preceded me in the East had a tendency to try and do everything themselves. Not having the time or knowledge to do it all myself, while I was a warden — and particularly as master — I formed committees, and I delegated many duties and responsibilities to the other officers and new members, to get them involved and active in the Lodge.

Now, as another "has been" Past Master on the sidelines, I try to get to know all new members and reach out to those who are slipping into "part time" status, to keep them feeling welcome and engaged. Recently, a great device was dropped into my lap: I was asked to revive our Fellowcraft team, which has been inactive longer than I have been a Mason.

The Successful Lodge

I am using this opportunity to involve some new and less-active Masons, and to get them involved and socializing with other members of the Lodge during practices and social meetings of the team.

We are also doing some renovations and updating of the public spaces of our building. We have incorporated the talents and energy of some of our newer members to lead and execute the project.

We have teamed up with a couple of local Scout troops to assist with their Eagle Scout projects. We believe that having the Scouts and their parents around the Lodge and our members is great way to introduce the next generation of "good men" to Masonry. We are also attempting to incorporate more family functions into our calendar, to get wives and families involved and participating with the Lodge.

For me, making the Brothers — and their families — feel welcome and actively wanting to participate in *all* activities is what makes a Lodge grow and become successful.

R. WESLEY WEBBER
PDDGM/PM, William McKinley #431

What makes a Lodge successful?

A successful Lodge is one with friendly men who care about one another, want to do things together, and rally to the Lodge's causes. Membership numbers do not count as much as the number of members who stand up to be counted.

What is necessary to have a successful Lodge?

It is necessary to have leaders of each age cohort that are interested in preserving Masonry. Those of us that are Social Security-eligible may be of some historical interest to the 20-something Masons, and perhaps may be able to mentor a few who are good listeners. Otherwise, we need to empower the youth to steer the craft and reach their peers with the message tailored to their generation. Masonry has many aspects that can reach into a man and uplift him. Each generation needs its own spokesmen.

How do you make a Lodge successful?

If a Lodge is not on the path to success, it will take leaders within the Lodge to have a "come to Jesus" meeting and create a buzz and have a revival of spirit. Commitment to the present officers and a grooming of the next line officer candidates is necessary on the part of the Past Masters and Past LEOs. Men who are not made to feel welcome do not return. Install a greeter system like at a church. Make him welcome, sit with him, and follow up the next week to see if he needs a ride to the next meeting.

Old Portage Temple, January 2015. By Easterling.

DAN WELCH
PM, Port Washington #202

What makes a Lodge successful?

Lack of debt, for one.

Stability in its leadership, two.

And having the right Brothers, who will try something new and see it through.

What is necessary to have a successful Lodge?

Well, we know we need money.

We need to be proud of our Lodges and not take them for granted.

How do you make a Lodge successful?

Obviously, you need a *good* secretary!

I've said for a long time: We have to offer them something they can't get somewhere else. I have dealt with people in business all of my adult life, and for the most part, people have changed: Many people have forgotten about loyalty, and are selfish, and think "It's all about me" and live paycheck to paycheck.

To be successful, we need new members and new ideas. I think it starts from the top. Our district had trips to Washington, D.C. and Put in Bay, and they were awesome! We staged a trip to Wheeling Island a few years ago. That was successful, but none of the masters after that kept it going. That particular master put that trip together with his own money did the legwork himself — and the ball got dropped. To be quite frank, to answer the question: HARD WORK, DEDICATION, AND LOVE OF THE FRATERNITY!

Let me ask you a question:

How do you make a Brother love the fraternity?

If we can find this answer, problem solved!

TOM WHITE
PDDGM/PM, Canton #60

What makes a Lodge successful?

What is necessary to have a successful Lodge?

How do you make a Lodge successful?

There are two words that are common to all three of the above questions: Lodge and successful. Let's assume "Lodge" means the entity that is formed by a group of Masons. However, I think we should define the meaning of "success" before we answer the questions.

There are many ways to define success. If it means the number of members, then Lodges with the highest number of members are the most successful.

Are Lodges that can pay their bills on time with income produced by members' dues successful?

If a Lodge consistently has a majority of its members present at their stated and special meetings, are they successful?

Does a successful Lodge provide stimulating and thought-provoking discussions and programs for its members?

Can a Lodge that is active and visible in their community be described as successful?

Can a Lodge be successful if they have only a few Brothers who are willing to assume office, and those Brothers just rotate through the chairs over and over again?

127

The Successful Lodge

Is a Lodge successful if they raise one candidate, or 20, to the Sublime Degree of Master Mason?

Does a Lodge with a large amount of money meet the definition of success?

Can I make a Lodge successful by paying my dues on time?

Will my Lodge be successful if I accept appointment as an officer?

Is my Lodge a success if I donate money to its charities?

Will my Lodge be successful if I help with the maintenance of the physical property?

If I visit our distressed and ill Brothers, will my Lodge be successful?

Am I doing all I can to exhibit the qualities of Brotherly Love, Relief and Truth, so that others will want to become a member of my Lodge?

Do I talk about the great meetings and meaningful contributions my Lodge is engaged in to everyone I come in contact with?

There are many more questions that can be raised about what makes a successful Lodge. And I believe that the answers can be found in the questions we ask.

Every Lodge and every Lodge Brother can and will be successful if he can answer these and any other questions with a positive and meaningful answer that reflects what he is doing as a Mason.

JEFF WINTERS
WM, Hudson #510

What makes a Lodge successful?

A commitment by the leadership and Brethren to continuous improvement in all aspects of the Lodge.

What is necessary to make a Lodge successful?

Lodge officers providing real leadership, while at the same time building the trust and respect of the Brethren.

How do you make a Lodge successful?

• A strong officer line.

• Setting goals and steps to achieve them.

• Being more particular in choosing candidates for the officer line. Don't rush new members into the line; observe them for awhile, to see if they have the qualities of good leadership.

• Ask members to be more involved. Let them pick what they would enjoy doing, rather that just assigning.

• Build teamwork by insisting on good degree work, and by keeping committees working on their goals. This builds cooperation and improves results.

• Keep community visibility and activities high. This builds respect for Masonry and attracts new recruits.

• Resolve conflicts quickly.

• Ask often and thank often.

• Adequate fundraising efforts.

• Communicate, communicate, communicate.

• Make time to have some fun, but make sure the sum total of time spent on Masonry does not burn out a Brother's enthusiasm — or his family's patience.

NICK WLADYCZAK
SS, Wayfarer #789

What makes a Lodge successful?

A fun environment, and a group of guys that like having fun. An environment that the family can get involved in, also.

What is necessary to have a successful Lodge?

A happy and thriving membership. Activities that involve the entire family.

How do you make a Lodge successful?

You can't make a Lodge successful; it has to be done through a committed leadership. Activities that keep new members involved — and depending on the area, these activities can vary greatly!

You honestly can't grow membership without a strong core that does things outside of Lodge. Look at the Alliance Shrine Club, for example. They get together all of the time, and they have a growing membership because of it. They all hang out at the same place, and are always doing things together that range from a moonlight golf to a singing memorial dinner. They have fun and can be serious. But most importantly, they are friends outside of Masonic organizations!

Portage Lakes Temple.
February 2015. Photo by Easterling.

JAMES YOCUM
PDDGM/PM, Wayfarer #789

Planning!

Successful Lodges have an active and interested Master, who promotes quality ritual work, keeps members (especially officers) active and interested by scheduling ritual practices, and as many social events during his year as possible.

Lodge members — officers especially — should take their wives or significant other to as many dinners and events as possible to make them feel that they are part of Masonry. It makes it a little easier for you to get away a few nights a week.

Lack of planning is evident when we ask for the District 21 form for the inspection and installation schedule. Until the last minute, many senior wardens are simply not prepared to provide that information — and then they only pull it together after their feet are held to the fire.

Come September, when we ask a Lodge secretary for information, the answer, too many times, is that the senior warden has not told him, and it is too early to provide the names of officers for the upcoming year, as well as event dates. It is simply a lack of planning earlier in their year as senior warden.

The Lodge secretary is in the best position of all to help the incoming master and the Lodge. He should guide and help him plan his year — which does not mean he should spend his time running the Lodge.

I think it is part of the Lodge secretary's responsibility to strongly encourage the senior warden to start planning his year over the summer break. I make a list of things that the senior warden should be thinking about. And come September, I look for some answers. A pain in the neck to some, but most thank me come October.

District educational seminars for the Master and officers down through the deacons would be helpful. They should be kept short and informative — and perhaps combined with a dinner or other social event.

JOHN W. YOUNG
JW, Victory #649

What makes a Lodge successful?

Communication.

What is necessary to have a successful Lodge?

Commitment.

How do you make a Lodge successful?

By not lacking in either of the above.

THE SUCCESSFUL LODGE

TOM ZAHLER
PM, Clinton #47
<u>**Past Grand Master, Grand Lodge of Ohio, F. & A.M.**</u>

What makes a Lodge successful?

I believe that, to attain a successful Lodge, the officers and members have to enjoy the fellowship of working together. They need to plan social events that include the entire family, whether they be inside or outside the Lodge.

A few possibilities: A family night at a local theater. Or perhaps a short weekend trip to visit a famous landmark. Or maybe a water park where the children will enjoy themselves.

The problem lies with lazy or ineffective officers who will not sacrifice the time to set up this kind of event.

A Lodge can only be a successful vehicle if those who are driving it know where they're going!

What is necessary to have a successful Lodge?

To have a successful Lodge, I feel, requires similar responsibilities — mainly to the corps of officers who must learn the ritual work they are assigned to at their stations, who show the membership that they are proud to represent the Lodge.

There should be a committee of Brethren and/or widows of deceased members.

A newsletter from the Lodge should inform the Lodge of events coming up in the future. And hopefully some of the programs will somehow include community projects, to ensure a positive impression in their area.

How do you make a Lodge successful?

How to make a Lodge successful is the question of the ages, because if they are unable to locate good men for officers, and they can only find some "old timers" who are willing to keep the seat warm, they're behind the eight ball from the get-go.

In some instances, before a Lodge and building become ineffective, they might consider merging with another Lodge, and maybe become revitalized. Individual Masons are more important than a Lodge name and number.

NOTES

Richfield Temple, January 2015. By Easterling.

James F. Easterling, Jr.
Past Grand Master of Masons in Ohio (2012-2013).
Photo by Brother Warren Gregory.

ABOUT THE AUTHORS

James F. Easterling, Jr., is a Past Grand Master of Masons in Ohio and a Thirty-Third Degree Mason of the Ancient & Accepted Scottish Rite. Brother Easterling is a member of National Lodge #568 in Ohio's 21st Masonic District, having served his Blue Lodge as Worshipful Master in 1996.

He is serving as National Lodge #568's fundraising chairman, and his Masonic résumé includes dozens of roles, including Portage Chapter #202 Royal Arch Masons, Akron Council #80 Royal & Select Masons, Akron Commandery #25, Tadmor Shrine, Widow's Sons Masonic Motorcycle Association, and the Honorary Member of the Order of DeMolay. He has served as Thrice Potent Master, Aroba Lodge of Perfection, AASR Valley of Akron; President of the Scottish Rite Officers Association, the Endowment Fund Committee, and currently Deputy's Representative. He was also his Blue Lodge's chaplain, trustee and a member of the Temple Board Committee.

He and his wife, Jill, are members of Bolivar Chapter of the Order of the Eastern Star.

David Ferris is WM of Meridian Sun Lodge #69, which was chartered in 1824. He is an Ohio Society of Professional Journalists Reporter of the year, and teaches at the University of Akron. A Scottish Rite Mason, he is editor of the Valley of Akron's *Rite Lite* newsletter, which won the Northern Masonic Jurisdiction's Outstanding Newsletter award. He enjoys talking shop about ritual and memorization.

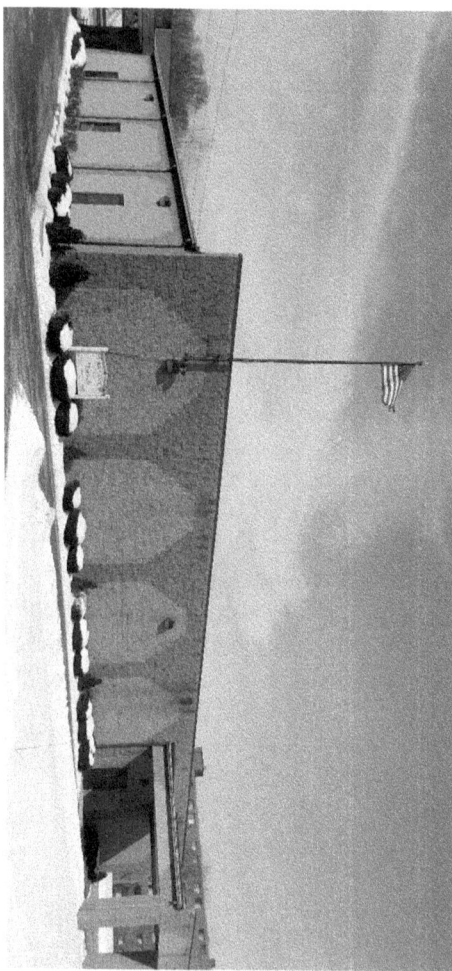

Massillon Temple, March 2015. By Easterling.

Strasburg Temple, February 2015. By Easterling.

Freemasonry: A Way of Life
Truncated from a pamphlet by The Grand Lodge of Ohio

The fraternity of Free and Accepted Masons is the oldest, largest, and most widely known fraternal organization in the world.

Members of the Masonic Fraternity come from virtually every occupation and profession — from all stations in life. Fourteen U.S. Presidents have been proud to be counted as Brothers, as have five Chief Justices and scores of governors, senators, and congressmen. Leaders from all walks of life and all corners of the globe have sought Masonic membership.

All Masons meet on an equal basis as friends, regardless of income, political ideology, or religious belief. All believe in a Supreme Being and are all patriotic citizens who obey the governments under which they live.

One of the customs of Freemasonry is not to solicit members. When someone petitions membership, it is of his own free will and accord. They must ask a Mason for a petition. Masons are most willing to answer questions and share information with those who are not members, and will enthusiastically assist anyone indicating a willingness to petition for membership. In Ohio, a Mason must be 19 years old, of good moral character, and believe in the existence of a Supreme Being.

Masonry was founded on the principles of Brotherly Love, Relief, and Truth, and takes seriously its responsibility to help others. The Masonic fraternity in the United States *daily* contributes more than $1.2 million to charitable causes.

Visit www.Freemason.com to learn more.

Directory of
Ohio's 21ˢᵗ Masonic District
"To be one, ask one."

Lodge: Clinton #47
Street address: 333 2nd St SW
                   Massillon, Ohio 44646
Phone number: 330-833-7615
Email contact: clintonLodge47@gmail.com
web address: www.ClintonLodge47.com
Meetings held: 2nd & 4th Tuesdays
Date chartered: June 22, 1837

Tuscarawas #59
735 N. Wooster Ave
Dover, Ohio 44622
330-364-3231
mail@TuscLodge59.com
www.TuscLodge59.com
1st & 3rd Wednesdays
December 11th, 1821

Canton #60
836 Market Ave N
Canton, Ohio 44702
330-455-6300
www.Canton60Freemasons.com
1st & 3rd Wednesdays
December 11th, 1821

Meridian Sun #69
4586 Streetsboro Rd
Richfield, Ohio 44286
330-659-9526
jegto@windstream.net
www.MeridianSun.org
1st & 3rd Wednesdays
January 14th, 1824

Coventry-Akron #83
3000 Krebs Dr. Suite C
Akron, Ohio 44319
330-644-5828
coventryakron@att.net
1st Thursday
October 20th, 1841

New Philadelphia #177
202 West High St. New Philadelphia, Ohio 44663
330-339-6442
www.NewPhila177.org
1st & 3rd Mondays
October 16th, 1841

Star #187
2307 Sacket Ave. Cuyahoga Falls, Ohio 44223
330-923-3714
eteldest@yahoo.com
www.facebook.com/StarLodge187
2nd Monday
October 16th, 1850

Mystic Tie #194
415 Center St. Dennison, Ohio 44621
330-364-3231
1st and 3rd Mondays
October 17th, 1850

Port Washington #202
112 South Walnut St. Gnadenhutten, Ohio 44629
740-254-9366
2nd & 4th Mondays
October 25th, 1851

Summit #213
9545 Shepard Rd. Twinsburg, Ohio 44087
330-467-7775
secretary@summit213.org
www.Summit213.org
1st & 3rd Thursdays
October 27th, 1851

Conrad #271
144 S. Linden Ave. Alliance, Ohio 44601
330-823-5181
conradLodge@att.net
www.ConradLodge.org
1st and 3rd Tuesdays
October 25th, 1855

Caldwell #330
11150 Glenpark Dr NE / Bolivar, Ohio 44612
330-874-3144
caldwell330@freemason.com
www.facebook.com/CaldwellLodge330
1st & 3rd Saturday
October 18th, 1860

William McKinley #431
836 Market Ave North / Canton, Ohio 44702
330-455-6300 • trundquist@yahoo.com
www.McKinley431freemasons.com
2nd & 4th Fridays
October 20th, 1869

Twinsburg Temple, January 2015. By Easterling.

Hudson #510

49 East Streetsboro Street
Hudson, OH 44236
330-650-4554
HudsonLodge510@yahoo.com
HudsonLodge.org
1st Monday, 7:30 p.m.
October 18th, 1876

Adoniram-Joppa #517

3000 Krebs Dr. Room A
Akron, Ohio 44319
330-208-2398
517adjo@gmail.com
2nd Monday, 7:30 p.m.
October 16th, 1878

Tubal #551

133 Bonnieview Ave
Minerva, Ohio 44657
330-205-2158
2nd & 4th Tuesdays, 7:30 p.m.
October 23rd, 1889

National #568

107 5th St NW
Barberton, Ohio 44203
330-745-4920
www.National568masons.net
1st Tuesday, 7:30 p.m.
October 19th, 1893

Cypress #604
Street: 140 South Bodmer Ave.
Mail: P.O. Box 121
Strasburg, Ohio 44680
330-878-7080
1st & 3rd Wednesdays, 7:30 p.m.
October 21, 1909
Strasburg, Ohio 44680

Ashlar #639
9545 Shepard Rd
Twinsburg, Ohio 44087
phone: 330-612-5018
FAX: 330-779-8223
oh639poobah@windstream.net
www.AshlarLodge639.com
2nd Wednesday, 7:30 p.m.
October 18th, 1917

Victory #649
1009 Kenmore Blvd. Akron, Ohio 44314
330-510-1009
Victory649@yahoo.com
www.Victory649.org
2nd Tuesdays, 7:30 p.m.
October 16th, 1919

Mount Akra #680
1589 Akron Peninsula Rd
Akron, Ohio 44313
330-929-9165
1st Monday, 7:30 p.m.
October 19th, 1922

Trinity #710
836 Market Avenue North
Canton, Ohio 44702
330-455-6300
sdenayer@sbcglobal.net
1st & 3rd Thursdays, 7:30 p.m.
October 22nd, 1931

Cuyahoga Falls #735
2307 Sackett Ave. Cuyahoga Falls, Ohio 44223
330-923-3714
skeenancf735@gmail.com
www.facebook.com/CuyahogaFalls735
1st Wednesday, 7:30 p.m.
October 18th, 1951

Barberton #750
4395 Rex Lake Rd
Akron, Ohio 44319
330-745-1317
tracynscott@gmail.com
2nd & 4th Wednesdays, 7:30 p.m.
October 17th, 1953

Stow #768
2307 Sackett Ave
Cuyahoga Falls, Ohio 44223
330-688-4042
rmcmillan1@neo.rr.com
2nd & 4th Tuesdays, 7:30 p.m.
October 13th, 1962

William H. Hoover #770
805 Orchard Ave NE
North Canton, Ohio 44720
330-499-9830
www.NorthCantonmMasons.org
1st & 3rd Tuesdays, 7:30 p.m.
October 21, 1966

Wayfarer #789
4395 Rex Lake Rd
Akron, Ohio 44319
330-644-9711
jyocum@neo.rr.com
www.WayfarerLodgeNo789.com/
1st Wednesday, 7:30 p.m.
September 9th, 2006

Northeast Ohio is not always a land of ice and snow.
The view from Craftsman Park in Portage Lakes,
Ohio. Photos by Easterling.

CRAFTSMEN PARK:
One of the 21st Masonic District's Jewels

Open to Brethren and their families, Craftsmen Park was formed in 1933, as a 501(c)(3) nonprofit organization, sponsored by members of the Free & Accepted Masons of Ohio residing in Summit County, Ohio. It was to be used for camps for children, teaching moral and ethical skills needed to become good citizens and productive members of society.

In 1948, Craftsmen Park purchased the property it now occupies on the shores of Rex Lake. Comprising 68 acres, this property gave the Masonic Fraternity the flexibility to expand and serve other organizations interested in the welfare of our youth. Today this includes the Boy Scouts of America, school band camps, church groups, Rotary International, Camp Quality, Capstone Masonic Youth Camp and the Masonic Model Student Assistance Program, as well as the Masonic Boys and Girls Camps.

Funding to support the park comes primarily from the generosity of the Masonic Fraternity of Summit County and individual private donations. These funds are primarily used to provide for the operation and maintenance of the park and it facilities. Additional funds are raised through fundraisers like our dinners and pancake breakfasts, and facility rentals for weddings and family outings. With continued support of the Masonic fraternity and the generosity of others, Craftsmen Park will continue to make its facilities available to organizations dedicated to the education and welfare of our most valuable asset, our youth.

Courtesy www.CraftsmenPark.com

James F. Easterling, Sr., National Lodge #568.

DEDICATIONS

James F. Easterling, Jr. thanks…

My father, James F. Easterling, Sr., for showing not only
me the way to join this great Fraternity, but
my brother Jeff, brother-in-law Randy, and nephew Kyle,
all of whom are members of National Lodge #568.

WB Dave Ferris, for all of his help on this project.

Brethren of National Lodge #568.

WB Glen Wiseman, PM of Loyalty Lodge #645, who was
always there for encouragement as I became an officer.

The Brethren who took time out of their day
to contribute to this project.

RWB Tom White.

David Ferris thanks…

MW Brother James F. Easterling, Jr.

All the Brethren who shared their knowledge and time.

Bob Becker and the Past Masters of Meridian Sun #69.
Our fellow officers, past and present.
Kevan Hudak, Karen Wilson, and our dedicated families.

George Seabeck, 33°, Associate Grand Chaplain.

Jim Himmelright, 33°, Valley of Akron.

Northern Light Editor Alan Foulds, 32°.

Aimee E. Newell, Ph.D., Director of Collections,
Scottish Rite Masonic Museum & Library.

Rachel, Ryley, and Sydney. Love is like a rock.

Sumner J. Ferris, J. Budd Grebb, Ronald L. Forsythe RIP.
Veritas et Lux

Tadmor Shrine, January 2015. Photo by Easterling.

INDEX

THE
EASTERLING FOUNDATION SCHOLARSHIP APPLICATION

Send completed application to…

Easterling Scholarship
c/o Jim Easterling
P. O. Box 1137
Norton, Ohio 44203

Contact:
jimjr1137@neo.rr.com
mike@magic568.com

**21st District Easterling Scholarship Application
Due to District Chairman March 1st**

(For Committee use only): App. #_____

Personal Information:

Last Name _____
First Name _____ **Middle** _____

Home Address _____
_____

City/State/Zip _____

County _____
Date of Birth _____

Home Phone _____
E-mail _____

Mother's, Father's, or legal guardians address (if different from above)

_____

_____

General Information:

Please include a letter of recommendation

GPA, Attested by High School Counselor:_____

Name of accredited school to be attended:

_____

Are you related to a member of the Masonic fraternity?   _____ Yes _____ No

Name of relative   _____
Lodge#   _____

Financial:

Adjusted gross income reported to IRS previous year?

_____

Primary means of paying for college, including whether you will be working:

_____

Number of siblings living at home and their ages:

_____

_____

Name of Father/guardian:

_____

Occupation: _____

Name of mother/guardian:
_____
Occupation: _____

School related activities you participate in (clubs, sports, etc.)
_____
_____

Masonic related organizations you belong to (name and location): _____
_____

Community service or volunteer work:
_____
_____

Please write a brief essay on why you are attending college or vocational school. One page, double spaced, Times New Roman #12.

For bulk copies of this book and fundraising opportunities for your Lodge, please contact the publisher or authors: 6623Press@gmail.com or jimjr1137@neo.rr.com.